Updating Files

Purpose	Assistant Commands	
Add records	Update/Append	APPEND
Edit records	Update/Edit	EDIT
Browse records	Update/Browse	BROWSE
Replace specific field data	Update/Replace	REPLACE
Mark specific records for deletion	Update/Delete	DELETE *or* Ctrl-U while in Edit or Browse
Unmark specific records for deletion	Update/Recall	RECALL *or* Ctrl-U while in Edit or Browse
Purge marked records	Update/Pack	PACK

Positioning

Purpose	Assistant Commands	Dot Prompt Command
Find record quickly, using index	Position/Seek	SEEK *expression* (Use quotes around Character fields.)
Find record in unindexed database	Position/Locate then Retrieve	LOCATE
Move to next record while locating	Position/ Continue	CONTINUE
Move pointer ahead skipping one record	Position/Skip	SKIP
Move pointer to record specified by number	Position/Goto Record	GOTO RECORD

The Up & Running Series from SYBEX

Other titles include Up & Running with:

- **AutoSketch 3**
- **Carbon Copy Plus**
- **Clipper 5.0**
- **DOS 3.3**
- **DOS 5**
- **DR DOS 5.0**
- **Excel 3 for Windows**
- **Flight Simulator**
- **Grammatik IV 2.0**
- **Harvard Graphics**
- **Harvard Graphics 3**
- **Lotus 1-2-3 Release 2.2**
- **Lotus 1-2-3 for Windows**
- **Lotus 1-2-3 Release 2.3**
- **Lotus 1-2-3 Release 3.1**
- **Mac Classic**
- **Norton Utilities**
- **Norton Utilities 5**
- **Norton Utilities on the Macintosh**
- **PageMaker 4 on the PC**
- **PageMaker on the Macintosh**
- **PC Tools Deluxe 6**
- **PC-Write**
- **PROCOMM PLUS**
- **PROCOMM PLUS 2.0**
- **Q&A**
- **Q&A 4**
- **Quattro Pro 3**
- **Quicken 4**
- **ToolBook for Windows**
- **Turbo Pascal 5.5**
- **Windows 3.0**
- **Windows 286/386**
- **Word for Windows**
- **WordPerfect 5.1**
- **WordPerfect Library/ Office PC**
- **XTreeGold 2**
- **Your Hard Disk**

Computer users are not all alike. Neither are SYBEX books.

We know our customers have a variety of needs. They've told us so. And because we've listened, we've developed several distinct types of books to meet the needs of each of our customers. What are you looking for in computer help?

If you're looking for the basics, try the **ABC's** series, or for a more visual approach, select **Teach Yourself**.

Mastering and **Understanding** titles offer you a step-by-step introduction, plus an in-depth examination of intermediate-level features, to use as you progress.

Our **Up & Running** series is designed for computer-literate consumers who want a no-nonsense overview of new programs. Just 20 basic lessons, and you're on your way.

SYBEX **Encyclopedias** provide a comprehensive reference and explanation of all of the commands, features and functions of the subject software.

Sometimes a subject requires a special treatment that our standard series doesn't provide. So you'll find we have titles like **Advanced Techniques, Handbooks, Tips & Tricks**, and others that are specifically tailored to satisfy a unique need.

You'll find SYBEX publishes a variety of books on every popular software package. Looking for computer help? Help Yourself to SYBEX.

For a complete catalog of our publications:

SYBEX Inc.
2021 Challenger Drive, Alameda, CA 94501
Tel: (415) 523-8233/(800) 227-2346 Telex: 336311
Fax: (415) 523-2373

Up & Running with dBASE III PLUS®

Robert Cowart

SYBEX®

San Francisco ▪ Paris ▪ Düsseldorf ▪ Soest

Acquisitions Editor: Dianne King
Series Editor: Joanne Cuthbertson
Editor: Janna Hecker Clark
Technical Editor: Michael Warren
Word Processors: Ann Dunn, Susan Trybull
Book Designers: Ingrid Owen, Helen Bruno
Icon Designer: Helen Bruno
Screen Graphics: Cuong Le
Desktop Production Artist: Lucie Zivny
Proofreaders: Carolina Montilla, Catherine Mahoney
Indexer: Ted Laux
Cover Designer: Archer Design

Library of Congress Card Number: 91-75003
ISBN: 0-89588-886-6

Manufactured in the United States of America
10 9 8 7 6 5 4 3 2 1

Acknowledgments

Thanks to all the people at SYBEX who have made publishing with them so enjoyable. I specially want to thank my editor, Janna Hecker Clark; Acquisitions Editor Dianne King; Technical Editor Michael Warren; and Dr. Rudolf Langer for their assistance and encouragement.

Thanks also to the folks in the SYBEX Art department who typeset and laid out this book.

To my dad—the greatest guy I know.

SYBEX Up & Running Books

Who this book is for

The Up & Running series of books from SYBEX has been developed for committed, eager PC users who would like to become familiar with a wide variety of programs and operations as quickly as possible. We assume that you are comfortable with your PC and that you know the basic functions of word processing, spreadsheets, and database management. With this background, Up & Running books will show you in 20 steps what particular products can do and how to use them.

What this book provides

Up & Running books are designed to save you time and money. First, you can avoid purchase mistakes by previewing products before you buy them—exploring their features, strengths, and limitations. Second, once you decide to purchase a product, you can learn its basics quickly by following the 20 steps—even if you are a beginner.

Contents & structure

The first step usually covers software installation in relation to hardware requirements. You'll learn whether the program can operate with your available hardware as well as various methods for starting the program. The second step often introduces the program's user interface. The remaining 18 steps demonstrate the program's basic functions, using examples and short descriptions.

Special symbols and notes

A clock shows the amount of time you can expect to spend at your computer for each step. Naturally, you'll need much less time if you only read through the step rather than complete it at your computer.

You can also focus on particular points by scanning the short notes in the margins and locating the sections you are most interested in.

In addition, three symbols highlight particular sections of text:

The Action symbol highlights important steps that you will carry out.

The Tip symbol indicates a practical hint or special technique.

The Warning symbol alerts you to a potential problem and suggestions for avoiding it.

We have structured the Up & Running books so that the busy user spends little time studying documentation and is not burdened with unnecessary text. An Up & Running book cannot, of course, replace a lengthier book that contains advanced applications. However, you will get the information you need to put the program to practical use and to learn its basic functions in the shortest possible time.

We welcome your comments

SYBEX is very interested in your reactions to the Up & Running series. Your opinions and suggestions will help all of our readers, including yourself. Please send your comments to: SYBEX Editorial Department, 2021 Challenger Drive, Alameda, CA 94501.

Preface

Since its wide-spread acceptance in the early 1980s, dBASE has remained the industry standard for PC databases. The program dBASE III PLUS, although technically supplanted by dBASE IV in 1990, continues to hold its own as the most popular database management program for PCs. This is due in part, of course, to the millions of copies of dBASE III PLUS in use around the globe.

This book is designed to help you learn the rudiments of dBASE III PLUS quickly, without a lot of hand-holding. I've used examples throughout the 20 steps to illustrate the concepts I discuss.

With dBASE III PLUS you can easily manage small to large amounts of information—whether textual, logical (true/false), or numeric. Once input, you can easily organize, delete, insert, modify, extract, or update your information, as well as create a wide variety of printed reports, mailing labels, and mail-merged letters. You can also create custom screens for entering and retrieving your data.

We hope you like this book. If you have any comments or suggestions, please write to SYBEX. We are always happy to respond.

Table of Contents

15

Installing dBASE III PLUS

Before you can use dBASE III PLUS you must first register your copy of the software and install it on your computer. This is easily done using the ID (identification) and install programs supplied with dBASE. Step 1 describes these procedures.

PROTECTING YOUR dBASE III PLUS DISKS

To guard against damage to your original dBASE disks, be sure to make copies of both using either the DOS COPY command or the DISKCOPY command. (Refer to your DOS manual if you don't know how to format and copy disks.) Store the originals in a safe place. Use only your copies to run dBASE.

REGISTERING YOUR COPY OF dBASE III PLUS

1. Boot up your computer in the usual way.
2. Examine the label on the dBASE System Disk #1 to determine your serial number. Write this down on a piece of paper.

3. Insert System Disk #1 in drive A.
4. Log onto drive A. Run the program called ID by typing **ID** and pressing Enter. Enter the serial number of the program, your company name (if applicable), and your name in response to the prompts on the screen.

CHECKING YOUR CONFIG.SYS FILE

Note: If your computer has only 256K of RAM, disregard this section.

To install dBASE you must have a CONFIG.SYS file in the root directory of your boot disk. To determine if this file is present, switch to the boot disk and root directory (typically C:\ on a hard-disk system or A:\ on a floppy-disk system with the boot disk inserted in drive A), and at the DOS prompt type

```
dir config.sys
```

Press Enter.

Copying the CONFIG .SYS file

If you get the message “File not found,” you may copy the supplied CONFIG.SYS file on System Disk #1 to your boot disk using the DOS COPY command.

If you already have a CONFIG.SYS file on your boot disk, use the DOS TYPE command

```
type config.sys
```

to view the file. Check to see that it has the following settings:

```
FILES=15
BUFFERS=20
```

If you want to use your existing CONFIG.SYS file because it has other settings you want to keep, first make a backup copy, then edit

STEP 1

INSTALLING dBASE ON A HARD-DISK SYSTEM

RAM requirements

Before installing dBASE III PLUS on a hard disk, make sure you have at least 700K of space available. If your computer has only 256K of RAM in it, continue to the section "If Your Computer Has Only 256K of RAM" before you run dBASE.

Be sure to uninstall any existing copy of dBASE III PLUS before installing a new copy of dBASE III PLUS on your hard disk. Otherwise, versions may collide. Use the uninstall program supplied with the other version of dBASE to do this. Then follow these steps:

1. Follow the CONFIG.SYS file instructions above (unless you have only 256K of RAM).
2. Create a directory for dBASE. From the root directory, type

   ```
   md dbase
   ```

   and press Enter. If you neglect this step, dBASE will be installed into the root directory.
3. Log onto the new directory by typing

   ```
   cd dbase
   ```

   Press Enter.
4. Now insert System Disk #1 into drive A and log onto drive A.
5. Then type

   ```
   install c:
   ```

   and press Enter. Answer any questions or prompts. When the installation is finished, you'll be returned to the DOS prompt.
6. Remove the disk in drive A and put it away in a safe place. Now you're ready to go on to Step 2 of this book.

INSTALLING dBASE ON A FLOPPY-DISK SYSTEM

If your system has no hard disk, follow these instructions.

1. Check the CONFIG.SYS file as described above.
2. Unless you have a system with only 256K of RAM, skip to Step 2 of this book to start up dBASE. If you have only 256K of RAM, continue with this Step.

IF YOUR COMPUTER HAS ONLY 256K OF RAM

These instructions replace the CONFIG.SYS file instruction given earlier, and apply only to systems of 256K.

CONFIG.DB changes

If your computer has only 256K of RAM, you'll have to modify both your CONFIG.SYS file and the CONFIG.DB file, which is supplied with dBASE and adjusts the program so that it can operate within limited memory space. Follow these steps:

1. Replace your CONFIG.SYS file on your startup (boot) disk with the file named CONFI256.SYS supplied on System Disk #1. Use the DOS COPY command to do this. (Refer to your DOS manual if you don't know how to use the COPY command.)

   - On a hard-disk system, insert System Disk #1 in drive A and type

     ```
     copy  a:\confi256.sys  c:\config.sys
     ```

     Press Enter.

   - On a floppy-disk system, insert System Disk #1 in drive B and your startup disk in drive A. Then issue the command

     ```
     copy  b:\confi256.sys  a:\config.sys
     ```

     and press Enter.

If you want to keep your CONFIG.SYS file because there are other settings in it that you want to use, edit the existing CONFIG.SYS file to include the statements

```
FILES=20
BUFFERS=4
```

2. Next, replace the CONFIG.DB file on System Disk #1 (if running from floppies) or in your hard-disk dBASE directory with the CONFI256.DB file.

   - For a hard-disk system, insert System Disk #1 in drive A. If dBASE is in the C:\dbase directory, issue the command

     ```
     copy a:\confi256.db c:\dbase\config.db
     ```

     and press Enter.

   - For a floppy-disk system, put the copy of System Disk #1 in drive A and insert the original in drive B. Issue the command

     ```
     copy  b:\confi256.db  a:\config.db
     ```

     and press Enter.

   The CONFIG.DB file contains settings that dBASE uses each time you run it. These settings are different for a 256K system. The settings should look like this when the file is typed out:

256K system settings

```
COMMAND=ASSIST
STATUS=ON
BUCKET=1
GETS=35
MVARSIZE=3
HISTORY=10
TYPEAHEAD=10
```

Once the CONFIG.SYS and CONFIG.DB files have been modified, you can run dBASE as explained in the next Step of this book.

15

Getting Started

In this step, you'll learn how to start up dBASE and operate the Assistant, dBASE's user interface.

STARTING dBASE

How you start dBASE depends on whether you have a hard-disk or floppy-disk system.

To begin working with dBASE, boot up your computer and get to the DOS prompt. If you're in Windows, click on the DOS prompt icon in the Main group to get to a prompt or exit Windows and wait for the DOS prompt to appear.

Starting From a Hard-Disk Drive

If you've installed dBASE on a hard disk, switch to c:\dbase (the drive and subdirectory you used during installation) and type

```
dbase
```

Press Enter.

You can avoid having to change directories by including your dBASE directory in the DOS path statement in your AUTOEXEC.BAT file.

Starting from a Floppy-Disk Drive

Start up dBASE by inserting System Disk #1 in drive A. At the DOS A: prompt type

```
dbase
```

and press Enter.

In a few seconds you'll be instructed to insert System Disk #2 into the drive.

THE dBASE INTERFACE

Turning Off the Assistant

The dBASE startup and copyright screen now appears. Press Enter to advance to the dBASE Main menu. The dBASE *Assistant* should appear (see Figure 2.1). If you don't see the Assistant screen, type **ASSIST** and press Enter, or press F2. The Assistant is an optional user interface that makes using dBASE easier. The Assistant can be turned

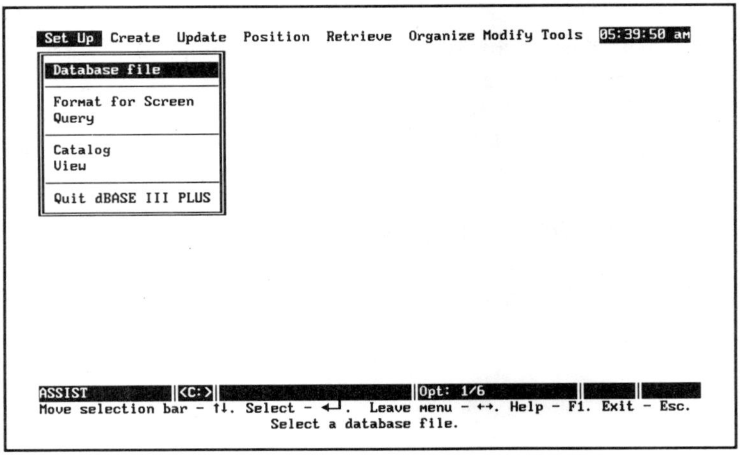

▪ *Figure 2.1: The Assistant opening screen*

off if you like, but then you have to type in complex commands at the dBASE *dot prompt*. Once you get familiar with dBASE commands, using the dot prompt can be a faster way to achieve the same results, however. For the purposes of this book, we'll assume you prefer to use the Assistant. However, we've included some exercises that use the dot prompt too, primarily for performing operations you can't achieve with the Assistant.

Menu names

The Assistant has eight menu names listed across the top of the screen. The Set Up menu is highlighted when you bring up dBASE. This means that the menu is open and that you can choose from the commands listed there. Press the → key to move the selection bar (highlight) to the right to highlight each of the eight menu names and see their associated lists of commands.

Each menu contains commands that have been grouped together because they have related functions. The purpose of each group is outlined below:

Set Up These commands open existing files and files that display data in predefined ways.

Create These options allow you to create new database files and other associated files, such as reports, mailing labels, and custom screen layouts.

Update Commands in this menu let you alter the actual information stored in your databases. This is in contrast to commands on the Modify menu, which are used to alter the database structure—the form in which the data appears on screen or on paper.

Position Use these commands to locate specific information in your database, such as a phone number.

Retrieve The commands in this menu allow you to list larger amounts of data, such as a report. Also for performing mathematical calculations such as summing or averaging.

Organize These commands are for rearranging the information in your databases. Used, for example, when sorting a list of customers by last name.

Modify Use these options to alter dBASE files, including the structure of existing databases, mailing label layouts, reports, custom screen displays, and queries.

Tools Use these commands primarily for performing DOS operations such as copying and erasing files, and logging onto other drives without leaving dBASE. Some DOS file commands, as well as a few dBASE-related commands, are on this menu. Also includes commands for importing and exporting files from and to dBASE.

You can quickly jump to another menu by pressing the first letter of its name.

Choosing Menu Commands

You choose a given command using the following steps:

1. Open the menu that contains the command.
2. Highlight the command, using the ↑ or ↓ key.
3. Press Enter.

The bottom line of the screen, called the *Message Line*, provides a brief description of the menu choice you have highlighted. Keep an eye on the Message Line for instructions.

Navigation Line instructions

Just above the Message Line is the Navigation Line. This line displays information about what moves you can make next and how to make them.

Immediately above the Navigation Line is the *Status Bar,* a highlighted line of information. This indicates the state of various optional settings, telling you whether you are using the Assistant, which disk drive your database files are on, whether your Caps Lock and Num Lock keys are on, and which option you are choosing from a menu.

The *Command Line* isn't evident until you begin building a dBASE command by making menu selections. To see the beginning of a Command Line, open the Create menu, highlight View, and press Enter. The Command Line should read:

```
Command: CREATE VIEW
```

For now, press Esc to back out of the command. If you press Esc too many times, though, you'll be at the dBASE dot prompt. If this happens, type **ASSIST** and press Enter (or press F2) to return to the Assistant.

If you can't highlight a menu choice, it means the commands on the menu aren't available to you at the moment because you are not working with a database. The unavailable choices are usually displayed in dimmer letters, also called ghost text.

Backing out of commands

If you decide, after choosing a command, that you want to back out of it, press the Esc key. This will usually take you back to the menu you were working with.

Getting Help When You Need It

On-line help

Sometimes you may need more help than is supplied by the Navigation and Message Lines. To get help on a subject, follow these steps:

1. Highlight the command you want help with.
2. Press the F1 key. A brief message about the command will appear on the screen. (Note that it may be cryptic or technical, since some of this information is designed for programmers.) A list of related topics will also be displayed.

3. Press Esc to clear the message and return to what you were doing.

EXITING dBASE

Whenever you are through working with dBASE, be sure to save your work and exit dBASE before turning off your computer. (The procedures for saving files are explained in future Steps.) Exiting dBASE is a simple process and one you should know now in case you want to take a break between Steps.

1. Open the Set Up menu.
2. Select Quit dBASE III PLUS.
3. Press Enter.

You'll be returned to the DOS prompt. You can now safely turn off your computer or work with another program.

30

Creating a Database

With the details of the Assistant under your belt you can now consider the essentials of creating a database. In this Step you'll learn how to create a new database from scratch, tailored to your data storage needs.

PLANNING YOUR DATABASE STRUCTURE

A database consists of a list of information and the form into which that information is put. The information is called the *data,* and the form is called the *structure.*

The first step in creating a new database is to decide what its structure should be. It's a little like drawing an empty form which will later be filled in with data. Start by considering what kind of data will be stored in the structure. This is best done by sitting down with a pencil and paper. Draw up a matrix, or table, that contains rows and columns. Your information will fit into these rows and columns. Each horizontal row is a *record,* and each column is a *field,* as you see in Figure 3.1.

Consider these questions:

- How do you want to enter the data?
- How many fields do you need?

Field # 1	2	3	4	5
check no.	description	charges	credits	balance
(record) # 1 # 2 # 3				

▪ ***Figure 3.1: A checkbook database***

- How will you want to retrieve the data?
- Will you need to organize the data by a particular field, such as last name?
- How long should each field be?
- What kind of data (letters, numbers, true/false, or dates) will go into each field?

Make notes for each of these questions and refer to them while following the instructions below. Here are the steps to take once you have come to some decisions:

1. Open the Create menu, highlight Database, and press Enter.

Command abbreviations

(From here on, we'll use a shorthand method to indicate menu choices. The preceding choice would be described as "Create/ Database." Each menu selection process is separated by a slash mark.)

2. A small box of drive names appears. Choose the drive where you want to store the database file you're creating, and press Enter. (If you are using a floppy-disk system, your database will be on drive B. Make sure you have a formatted floppy disk in that drive.)
3. Type in the file's name (up to eight characters, no extension necessary) and press Enter.

The database design screen now appears, as shown in Figure 3.2. This is where you specify the structure of a new database by filling in information about each field you want. The first field is waiting and ready to be defined.

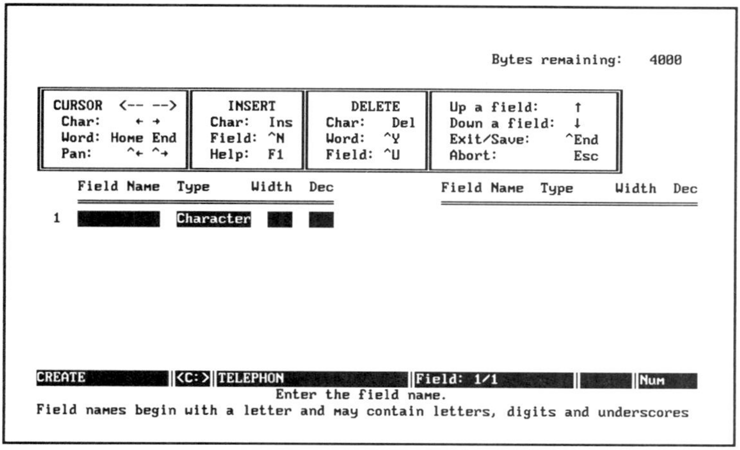

▪ *Figure 3.2: The database design screen*

Notice that there are four highlighted columns to be filled in:

```
Field Name    Type    Width    Dec
```

Here's the breakdown of what each of the columns means and what your options are for each one.

Field Name Each field needs to be named. Field names can be up to ten letters long (upper- or lowercase), and can contain only letters, digits, and underscores (_).

Type What kind of information is going to be stored in this field? The five choices are listed below. Make a selection by pressing the space bar until your choice appears.

Character—includes letters; punctuation marks; special symbols; and any numerals that are merely going to be printed, not used in mathematical calculations (zip codes, for example).

Numeric—numbers that will later require mathematical calculation, such as dollar amounts.

Logical—true/false or yes/no data, such as "did this person subscribe last year?" or "U.S. Citizen?"

Date—dates only, such as 12/5/93.

Memo—text about each record. For example, in a customer list you might want to have a Memo field so you can write a few notes about the customer's needs.

Conserving disk space

Width What is the maximum number of letters, numbers, etc., that you plan to put into the field? Only Character and Numeric fields require this setting—Logical, Memo, and Date fields are exempt. If you make a field too small, you will have to abbreviate long names or numbers to fit them into your database. If the field is too long, you will waste storage space on your disk.

Dec If the field you're defining is Numeric, indicate the number of decimal places you want it to accept and display. For standard monetary figures, you'd enter 2.

ENTERING THE FIELD INFORMATION

The next step is to enter the information about each field based on the decisions you made earlier.

1. The cursor is ready for you to type in the first field's name. Field names can be up to ten letters long. You can use the *underscore* character to separate words, but you can't use spaces. For example,

   `FIRST_NAME`

   is an acceptable field name.

Editing keys

2. Hit the Enter key to move to the Type column. (If the field name is ten characters or longer, the cursor jumps to the Type column by itself, and the computer beeps.) Press the spacebar to select the desired field type.

Use the ← key to back up to the previous column if you want to change the information you've entered. Other navigation and editing keys you can use while defining a database structure are in the upper half of the screen. The ^ represents the Ctrl key. When you see it, hold down the Ctrl key while pressing the indicated key.

3. Press Enter again to move to the Width column. Enter the width.
4. Unless your first field was a Numeric type, pressing Enter again moves the cursor down a line to the next field. If the field you were just describing was Numeric, you'll have to fill in the Dec field first by entering the number of decimal places you want displayed.
5. Continue entering the field descriptions you want in your database.

SAVING THE STRUCTURE

When you are through entering your field descriptions, press Ctrl-End as the Help box indicates (noted as ^End on the screen). Then follow these steps to save the database structure you've created:

1. The message line asks you to confirm that you wish to save the structure. Press Enter. The structure is stored on disk under the file name you supplied earlier.
2. The program now asks if you want to enter records:

   ```
   Input data records now? (Y/N)
   ```

   If you are ready to start adding data to your new database structure, enter Y. (As you may remember, data is the information you store in the database.) You are presented with the Append screen from which you enter your data. This is described in the Step 5 of this book. If you choose No, you are returned to the Assistant.

Changing the structure

If you are unhappy with the structure of your database, you will be able to change it. With certain limitations, this is possible even after you have added data records. You will learn how to modify the structure in Step 4.

15

Modifying a Database Structure

Often even the best-laid plans for creating a database structure are shortsighted. It's not an uncommon experience to find that the structure of your database needs alteration of some kind. Step 3 explained how to create a new structure. This Step will explain how to alter or modify it.

IDENTIFYING DATABASE STRUCTURE PROBLEMS

Fields too short or long

The most common changes people make to a database structure are adding or deleting fields, or changing field lengths. After typing in several records' worth of data, you may realize that you're using up precious disk space with fields that are too long or, conversely, that a field is too short and you can't get enough data into it. You may also realize that you omitted a necessary field—for example, a work phone number field in a phone book database.

Luckily, dBASE accommodates oversights by allowing you to modify an existing database structure (see Figure 4.1). It's even possible to change the structure after you have data in the file, though at that stage there are some restrictions.

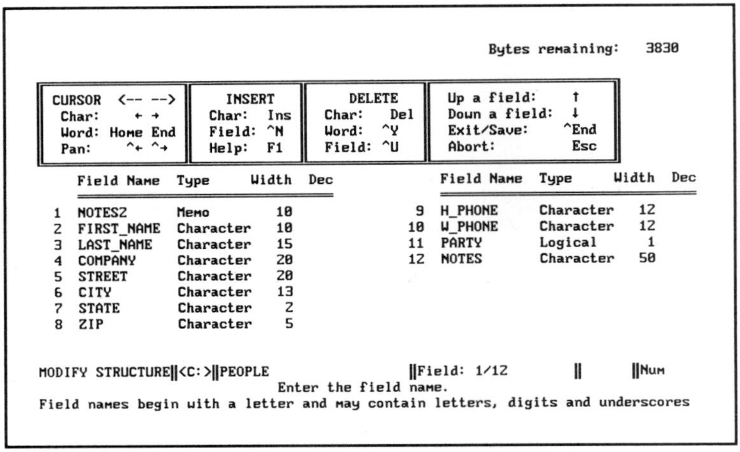

▪ *Figure 4.1: Modifying the Database Structure*

OPENING A DATABASE

Setting the default data drive

Before beginning to use databases and associated files that you've created and saved to disk, it's important to instruct dBASE where most of your files are stored. This is called *setting the default drive.* Setting the default drive saves you time by specifying in advance the location of your data files, so that you don't have to do so each time you go to open a file.

1. From the Assistant, choose Tools/Set Drive.
2. A box appears with drive letters. Highlight the correct drive and press Enter.

The selected drive is now the default drive and will be automatically selected whenever you attempt to save or open a file.

Modifying the structure of a database requires that you first open it. To open a database, follow these steps:

1. Choose Setup/Database File, select the drive letter (if necessary), and press Enter.

2. A list of files on the drive in the current directory will appear. Note that the extension *.dbf* will be added to files you saved in the past. Highlight the one you want to work with and press Enter.

.dbf extension

3. A box appears asking

   ```
   Is the file Indexed? [Y/N]
   ```

   The significance of this question will become clearer in later Steps, but for now simply type **N.**

The file is now in use. Any subsequent commands that you select from the menus will apply to that file. The database will stay in use until you open another one.

If you want to open a file in a directory other than the current one, you must do it from the dot prompt. You can't open such a file from the Assistant. To get to the dot prompt, exit the Assistant by pressing Esc a few times. The dot prompt (a period just above the Status Line) then appears. Enter the Use command followed by the full path name of the file. For example:

```
.use c:\projects\sales.dbf
```

Then type **ASSIST** and press Enter to return to the Assistant.

After opening the file, its name appears in the Status Line at the bottom of the screen.

MAKING ALTERATIONS

If you've already entered data into the database, be sure to read "Preserving Data When You Modify the Structure" at the end of this Step.

To remind yourself of the database's structure, you can use the Tools/List Structure command. Figure 4.2 displays a listing of an example database that stores phone numbers, addresses, and notes.

If you decide to modify the structure, choose Modify/Database File.

```
                                                          Num



. list stru
Structure for database: c:\people\people.dbf
Number of data records:      292
Date of last update   : 05/25/91
Field  Field Name  Type       Width    Dec
    1  NOTESZ      Memo          10
    2  FIRST_NAME  Character     10
    3  LAST_NAME   Character     15
    4  COMPANY     Character     20
    5  STREET      Character     20
    6  CITY        Character     13
    7  STATE       Character      2
    8  ZIP         Character      5
    9  H_PHONE     Character     12
   10  W_PHONE     Character     12
   11  PARTY       Logical        1
   12  NOTES       Character     50
** Total **                     171

.
```

■ *Figure 4.2: Database structure listing*

The same screen you used to create the database structure (see Figure 3.2) will now appear, listing the fields and allowing you to change the field names, sizes, and attributes. Use the editing keys listed in the boxes at the top of the screen to move between fields and make your alterations.

If you're working with a database that has lots of fields, press F1 to remove the help information on the upper half of the screen so that you can see more fields.

Inserting a Field

Ordering your fields

Before you add a new field, remember that when you type data into the database, the fields appear on the screen in the same order as they are in the structure. (This will become clearer as you begin entering data in Step 5.) Therefore, you'll probably want first names to be the first field, and last names to be the second field, like this:

```
1 FIRST_NAME
2 LAST_NAME
3 STREET
```

rather than in this order:

```
1 FIRST_NAME
2 STREET
3 LAST_NAME
```

To insert a field, do the following:

1. Use the arrow keys to place the highlight on the field where you want to make the insertion.
2. Press Ctrl-N. All subsequent fields will move down one row.
3. Enter the new field and its information.

Deleting a Field

To delete a field, do the following:

1. Use the arrow keys to place the highlight on the field you want to delete.
2. Press Ctrl-U. The field is deleted and all the subsequent fields will move up one row.

Changing Field Attributes

You can also change field names, types, lengths, and decimal places.

1. Using the Enter key to move between columns, position the cursor in the column containing the information you want to change. Keep your eye on the Message Line for helpful hints.
2. Change the Name, Type, Width, or Dec as needed.

SAVING THE MODIFIED STRUCTURE

When you're through modifying the structure you'll want to save the changes.

1. As the Help box on the screen advises, save and exit the modification process by typing Ctrl-End (^End).

2. The Message Line reads

   `Press ENTER to confirm, any other key to resume.`

   If you are not finished making changes, press any key other than Enter. If you want to save the changes, press Enter to do so. HOWEVER, IF YOU HAVE DATA IN THE DATABASE, YOU SHOULD TAKE A MINUTE TO READ AND UNDERSTAND THE NEXT SECTION FIRST! If you want to abandon the changes you've made and return to the previous state of the database, press Esc, then type **Y** in response to the prompt.

PRESERVING DATA WHEN YOU MODIFY THE STRUCTURE

As mentioned earlier, if you are careful you can modify the structure of a database even after it is filled with data. The process is the same as explained above, except for a few restrictions:

- Do not change more than one attribute per field at a time. For example, if you change a field's name, do not change its position at the same time. Conversely, if you change a field's length, do not change its name or position at the same time. Save the new structure first, with only one change. Then select Modify again and make the second change.
- Changing a field's type will cause data to be lost in that field.
- To change a field's position, first delete it from its current position, then insert a new field with the same name and characteristics in the desired position.

15

Entering Records

Step 4 explained how to fine-tune a database structure. This Step describes the various techniques for putting data in your database layout.

APPENDING RECORDS

Recall that data is stored in discrete records. Each record is like a paper form that you fill in with information. Records are separate entities that do not normally interact with each other. Thus, you'll have one record for each patient, client, account, inventory item, and so forth.

Appending is the process of adding data to an existing database structure. Assuming you have already successfully created and saved (and possibly modified) a database structure, you can begin entering your data—appending records.

1. If you did not modify the structure of your database, refer to Step 4 for instructions for setting the default drive. Select Tools/Set Drive and choose the drive that holds your data files.
2. Make sure you've opened the database file you want to work with, using the Setup/Database File command

(enter **N** at the index prompt unless you have created indexes, covered in Step 8, for the file).

3. Choose Update/Append. The program presents you with a blank form (see Figure 5.1) waiting to be filled in with the first record. Notice the similarities between this screen and the screen used to create and modify the database structure. The screens work similarly, but now you're entering data rather than entering the structure.

4. The cursor is positioned on the first field of the record. Note that the Status Bar indicates that you are in the Append mode. It also reports, to the right, the number of records in the database. If the database is new, the line reads

   ```
   Rec: None
   ```

   meaning there are no records.

5. To the left of the cursor you see the field names you chose when creating the structure. Each field name on the left is paired with the blank field space to its right. Begin entering your data in the first field. When it's typed in, press the

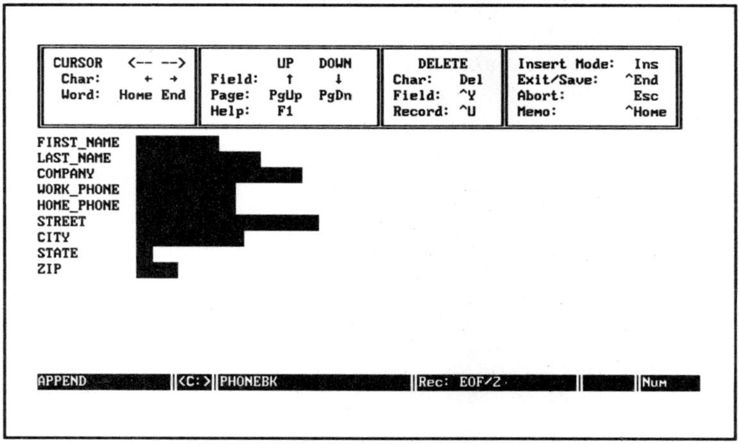

▪ *Figure 5.1: A blank record waiting to be appended to the database*

Enter key to move down to the next field, and repeat the process. You can fix mistakes by using the Backspace key. (Other editing keys are covered later.)

6. When you hit Enter after the last field, a new blank record comes up. Now you have the option of typing in the next record. The Status Line changes to

   ```
   EOF/2
   ```

   which means "End of File, you're on record number 2." *End of File* means you're currently on, or displaying, the last record in the file.

7. You can keep entering records in this manner until you run out of data. When you want to return to the Assistant, press Enter on the first field of a new record (don't type anything).

Of course, you can append new records at any time. They are just added to the end of the file.

SAVING YOUR WORK

When adding records you should occasionally save your work to disk. Power failures, program bugs, hardware problems, or operator errors always pose the threat of data loss, so make frequent saving a regular habit.

How often you decide to save you work depends on you. If you would mind losing more than 30 minutes of time, then you should save every half hour. I tend to save every five minutes or so. Here's how to save your work when appending:

1. Finish entering a record.
2. Before moving to the next record, press Ctrl-End or Ctrl-W. (I prefer Ctrl-W because it's easy to remember—the *W* *writes* the data onto the hard disk.)

As an alternative to step 2, you can hit Enter to bring up a new blank record, then hit Enter again. This will save the records you've added and return you to the Assistant.

STEP 5

EDITING YOUR DATA

There are several special editing commands used for correcting mistakes as you type and for moving the cursor around within a record. Many of the editing effects can be achieved more than one way. Table 5.1 lists the commands and their effects.

Main Key	*Letter Key*	*Result*
Enter		Moves to next field
↓	^K	Moves to next field
↑	^E	Moves to previous field
→	^D	Moves one space forward
←	^S	Moves one space back
Home	^A	Moves to beginning of word
End	^F	Moves to end of word
^Y		Deletes from cursor to end of field
Del	^G	Deletes character at cursor
Backspace		Deletes character to the left
Ins	^V	Turns Insert mode on/off

Table 5.1: Editing commands for data entry

Editing shortcuts

If you are a SideKick or WordStar user, you may notice that many of the letter key codes are identical to those you are already familiar with. Notice that the letter keys for moving the cursor up, down, left, and right are arranged in a sensible diamond pattern (see Figure 5.2). This makes it easy to remember which way you are moving, though using these keys requires pressing the Ctrl key with the little finger of your left hand. Unfortunately, many computer manufacturers now place the Ctrl key next to the Spacebar instead of the A key, making it awkward to use.

Turning Off the Help Screen

If your database structure has lots of fields, they will not all fit on the screen at once. You will have to press PgDn to see the rest of the

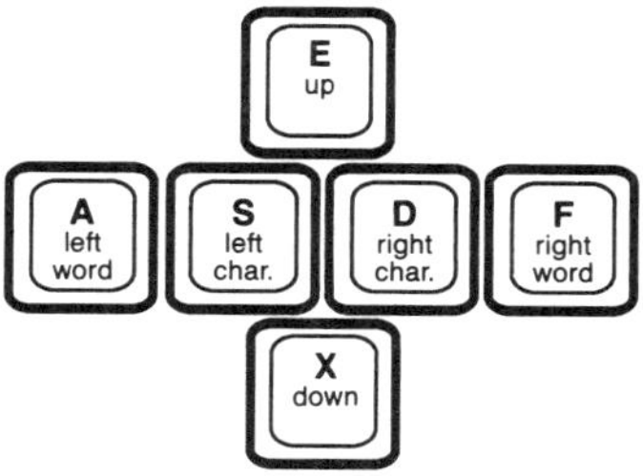

■ *Figure 5.2: The letter keys for cursor movement*

fields when entering your data. This can be a nuisance since it increases the key strokes required to enter information and doesn't allow you to see all the data in a record in one glance.

1. You can see more fields if you turn off the help information at the top of the screen by pressing F1.
2. When you need to see the help information, press F1 again.

The Insert Mode

Inserting text

Press Ins (or Ctrl-V) to switch to the Insert mode. Notice that "Ins" appears in the Status Line (in the second section from the right) to indicate the change. While in the Insert mode, characters you type are inserted into existing text, causing existing characters to be pushed to the right to make room.

Pressing Ins (or Ctrl-V) again turns the Insert mode off. Typing in a field that already has data in it will now overwrite that data with the new letters or numbers.

MAKING BACKUPS OF YOUR DATA

Don't underestimate the value of making backup copies of your databases. Both floppy and hard disks are delicate storage media, and it's not uncommon for a data file to be damaged in one way or another. The best protection against such an unhappy development is to make backup copies of your important files on a regular basis.

Backing up databases is as simple as using the DOS COPY command (when outside of dBASE) or the Copy command on the Assistant's Tools menu to place a copy of your *.DBF* files on a floppy. Usually, the files will fit on a floppy disk without modification. If you are working with large databases that will not fit, you may have to use the DOS BACKUP command or another such utility designed for backing up large files. Another approach with large files is to pack them using a utility such as ZIP or ARC, then copy the packed file onto a floppy.

30

Retrieving Your Data

Once you have stored data in a database using commands you learned in Step 5, you can begin experimenting with ways to retrieve and manipulate it. You can retrieve your data in two ways: dBASE can show you everything in the database, or you can request information that meets specified conditions. In either case, the process is called *querying* the database.

Querying the database

LISTING ALL THE RECORDS IN YOUR DATABASE

You can request to see all fields for all records, or selected fields for all records.

Listing All Fields

The simplest technique for looking at all the information in your database is to use the Retrieve/List command.

1. Open the database you want to look at.
2. Choose Retrieve/List.

3. A new box listing additional options appears to the right of the menu. "Execute the Command" is highlighted. Simply press Enter.

4. The Assistant asks if you want to send the listing to the printer. Type **N**. Your data scrolls up the screen, probably in a somewhat disorderly fashion, depending on the number of fields in the structure.

Jumbled field listings

If there are many long fields, the text will wrap around, causing a visual jumble on the screen (see Figure 6.1). If you display only a few fields, each record can fit on one line and you'll be able to glean desired information more easily.

Listing Selected Fields

You can limit the display to show only a few fields of each record. This is useful in a number of situations. It's likely that you will want to see only certain information—say, sales figures for a specific region, or last names and phone numbers. Follow these steps to

```
 Set Up  Create  Update  Position  Retrieve  Organize Modify Tools  11:46:44 pm
Record#  FIRST_NAME LAST_NAME       COMPANY                 WORK_PHONE   HOME_PHONE
   STREET                 CITY          STATE ZIP
      1  Randolf     Robbins         Ralph Nicolby Inc.     415-555-1212 415-555-11
11 374 Tipplemeyer Ave.   Cornmont        CA     94709
      2  Hank        Davies          Bass-O-Matic           909-549-3787 909-398-25
63 333 33rd St.           West Goshen   SD     43312
      3  Adriator    Weguo           Rug Flox, Inc.         321-889-3674 321-883-98
21 158 Snorewell Blvd.    Sleepyhollow  CA     02587
      4  Aretha      Phillipson      Soulariums-R-Us        908-776-5298 908-337-81
94 999 Motor City Ave.    Detroit         MI     39482
      5  Randy       Batterydown     Voltaics Inc.          809-675-4532 809-777-33
00 495 Anode St.          Carbondale     IL     30129
      6  Nimrod      Neverburger     Bab's Fish N Chips     822-991-2861 822-675-45
00 77 Easy Street         Khozad          CA     89751
      7  Marcel      Phillip         Feline Frenzy          310-563-0987 310-265-75
60 456 Fresno St.         Paris           TX     55493
      8  Valerie     Kuletski        Literary Allusions     529-221-9480 529-559-73
00 451 Farenheit Ct.      Oakland         CA     95420
      9  MARIAN      DAVIES          CITY OPERA CO.         211-334-9876 211-411-61
11 344 MARKET ST          NEW YORK        NY     10021

ASSIST          |<C:>|PHONE              |Rec: 1/9        |      |Num
                  Press any key to continue work in ASSIST.
```

▪ *Figure 6.1: A listing using the Retrieve/List command*

STEP 6

constrict the fields displayed:

1. Select List/Construct a Field List.
2. Two new boxes appear (see Figure 6.2). The box on the left lists the names of all the fields in the database. The box in the middle reminds you of the size and type of the highlighted field. To select a field or series of fields for inclusion in a listing, just highlight each one and press Enter.
3. Press → or ← to leave the Field Names box. This takes the cursor back to the List Option box.
4. Select Execute the Command. If you want to print the listing, prepare your printer and answer Y at the

   `Direct the Output to the Printer? [Y/N]`

   prompt. Otherwise, answer N to see the listing on the screen only. Figure 6.3 shows an example of a screen listing of three fields from a name and address list.

Rearranging the printed fields

If you want the fields arranged differently, construct the field list in the desired order. The first field you select will display or print to

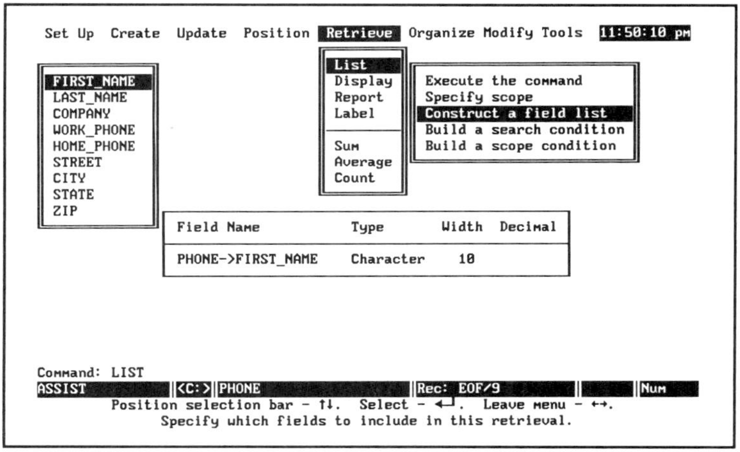

■ *Figure 6.2: Specifying a field list*

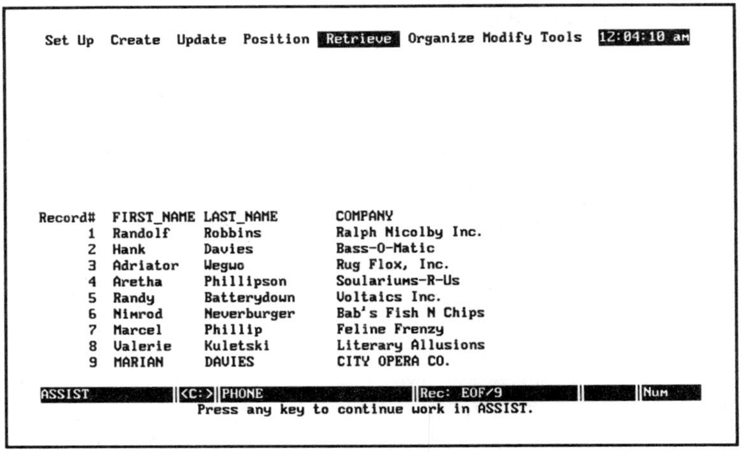

▪ *Figure 6.3: Listing of selected fields*

the far left, the next one adjacent to it, and so forth across the screen or paper.

LISTING ONLY SELECTED RECORDS

If you choose, you can list only those records that fulfill certain conditions.

Listing Records by Record Number

You will often want to retrieve specific records through the manipulation of, or reference to, their *record numbers*. The numbers in the leftmost column in Figure 6.3 are the record numbers of the displayed data. The program uses record numbers to keep track of your data in an orderly manner. Whenever you add a record to a database, it is automatically assigned a unique record number.

Record pointers

When working with dBASE it's important to understand that just as your eyes can read only one line of text at a time, dBASE can look at or work with only one record at a time. The record that dBASE is aware of, or currently positioned on, is monitored by a *record pointer.* The Status Line indicates the position of the pointer. For example, it may say

```
Rec: 89/129
```

which indicates that pointer is on record 89 of 129 records. The simplest way you refer to a particular record is by moving the pointer to that record's number. You can do this with the Position menu.

1. Select Position/Goto Record. A box appears.
2. Select Top, and the record pointer moves to the first record in the database. The record pointer indicates you are on record 1.
3. To display the record's contents, choose Update/Display or Update/Edit, depending on the format you want. Display shows all fields from left to right, whereas Edit displays them in the same format in which you entered them. (Edit also allows you to alter the contents of the fields, as explained in Step 9.)
4. To go to a record of a specific number, choose Position/Goto Record/Record and type in the record number. Then display or edit the record.

Using Record Numbers to Specify the Scope of a Listing

You may want to list several consecutive records. To do this, you specify the *scope,* or range, of the request by following these steps:

1. Position the pointer on the first desired record.
2. Select Retrieve/List/Specify Scope. (The program will not allow you to specify the scope if you're already at the end of the file.)
3. From the box that appears, choose Next. At the Numeric Value prompt, enter the number of records you want listed.
4. Execute the command.

You can combine a field list selection with a scope option. For example, you could choose to list only certain fields in only the next five records. To do this, first construct the field list. Then specify the scope and execute the command.

Listing Records That Meet Other Specified Conditions

Though it is sometimes useful to be able to list records by defining a scope, it's much more likely that you'll want to list the records whose field contents meet certain criteria. For example, you may want to list only those people whose addresses fall within certain zip code ranges, who live in California, or who work for a certain company. You do this by building a *search condition.*

Building search conditions

1. Decide which fields you want to include in the listing. Specify them using the Retrieve/List/Construct a Field List command (see "Listing Selected Fields").
2. If you want to limit your listing to a certain number of records, choose a scope for the listing.
3. Choose Build a Search Condition from the List submenu. A field list appears. Choose the field you want to base the search on, and press Enter. (For example, if your database has a field called STATE and you want to search for everyone living in California, choose STATE.)

Comparison operators

When you press Enter, another box appears, listing *comparison operators*. These are terms such as Equal To and Less Than. You use these operators to tell dBASE how to analyze the data in the field you've selected.

Though comparison operators are most often used for comparing numbers, they can be used with letters, too.

4. Choose the operator you want and press Enter. In our example, a search in your two-character long STATE field for California residents translates to a listing of all records where STATE = CA. Thus, you'd use Equal To.

5. Next, you are asked to

   `Enter a character string (without quotes):`

   Type in the comparison criteria and press Enter. For example, if you're looking for Jones, type in **Jones**. If you're looking for the number 2400, type that in.

Uppercase and lowercase letters are not considered by dBASE to be the same in search conditions. An "A" is not the same as an "a." Thus, a search for "jones" will not find "Jones." Be consistent about how you enter data into your databases so that searching can be done reliably later on. If you have no success listing a record that you know is in your database, don't give up. Try changing the case and executing the command again.

Uppercase and lowercase are not the same

6. Now another box appears, letting you enter additional criteria. You need to use additional criteria for complex searches such as "all accounts overdue *and* that have an outstanding balance of $2500." For simpler criteria based on one field, choose No More Conditions from the box and press Enter. (Searches based on multiple criteria are covered in Step 7.)

Multiple criteria searches

7. The Command Line displays the command as the Assistant has constructed it. Choose Execute The Command.

The program will list or print only the records that meet the criteria. If no records are displayed, you either entered the criteria incorrectly or no records meet the conditions you specified.

THE DISPLAY AND LOCATE COMMANDS

Another dBASE command, Display, is similar to List but adds two new features. The List command automatically scrolls data up and off the top of the screen when you have lots of data, making it difficult to view. The Display command shows only a screenful of data at a time. Pressing a key continues the display. The Retrieve/Display command can also be used to show only the record on which the pointer is currently positioned.

You can use the Display command to advantage with another command, Locate. Locate can be used to search for a particular record—say that of a specific client in your sales records. Once the desired record is located, the pointer remains positioned on it. You can then use Display to view the record's contents.

1. Choose Position/Locate.
2. Choose Build a Search Condition.
3. Select the field to search.
4. Choose a comparison operator.
5. Type in the search criteria.
6. Choose No More Conditions. (If you want to specify other conditions, refer to Step 7.)
7. Execute the command. The result is displayed above the Status Line. If no record was found, the message

   `End of Locate Scope`

   appears. If a record meeting the criteria was found, the record number is reported.
8. Choose Retrieve/Display/Execute the Command. The record's contents will be displayed in a linear fashion.

You can limit the fields you display by constructing a field list first. If you want to see the record in data-entry format, choose Update/Edit instead of Retrieve/Display.

30

Using Advanced Retrieval Techniques

Step 6 explained some simple approaches to retrieving information stored in your databases. This Step describes how to do more exacting data retrieval by combining search conditions, doing substring searches, and entering commands from the dot prompt.

COMBINING SEARCH CRITERIA

The last Step explained how to use the Equal To operator to search for a *string* of characters. Though you'll probably use this operator more than any other, it has its limitations. When trying to determine a range of acceptable data for displaying records, for example, you'll need to use another method. In this Step, you'll see how to do more complex searches using the combination box and dot prompt commands.

Combining Criteria with the .AND. Operator

Finding a range

Say you want to see all the records of people who live within a certain zip code range—for example, between 30129 and 60000. To retrieve this information, you must combine two criteria: for a record to qualify, its zip code must be both greater than 30129 and less than 60000. Recall from the Operator box that the following Comparison

Operators are available:

=	Equal To
<=	Less Than or Equal To
<	Less Than
>	Greater Than
>=	Greater Than or Equal To
<>	Not Equal To

To ferret out the range of records requested in this example, you must combine two criteria using the .AND. operator. Here's how:

1. If you want to limit the fields displayed, first construct a field list.
2. Select List/Build a Search Condition.
3. Choose the field on which you want to base the search (in this example, the ZIP field).
4. From the Operator box, choose > Greater Than.
5. Type in the lower range figure (for this example, it would be 30129).
6. Select Combine with .AND.
7. Choose the same field again from the field list.
8. From the Operator box, choose < Less Than.
9. Type in the higher range figure (for the example, 60000).
10. Choose No More Conditions.
11. Select Execute the Command.

Combining Criteria with the .OR. Operator

The other choice in the Combination box is Combine with .OR. This command lets you run searches for information like the names of all the people in your database who live in Illinois *or* in Texas.

You could do this by running two lists, one for each state, and using the Equal To operator. However, .OR. will do it faster. The technique is the same as described above for the .AND. operator—simply use .OR. instead of .AND.

.AND. and .OR., dubbed the *logical operators*, can be very useful when you are working with a large database. For example, say you want to look up a Sally Jones in your very large client database. Chances are good that your database contains more than one Sally and more than one Jones. You can avoid possible confusion by using the .AND. operator. Simply search for a first name of Sally and a last name of Jones.

ENTERING COMMANDS FROM THE DOT PROMPT

Despite its cleverness, the Assistant can sometimes be more trouble than it is worth. For experienced users, turning off the Assistant and using the dot prompt can be easier than making choice after choice from the menus. Also, there are some things the Assistant can't do.

Entering dot prompt commands

1. Leave the Assistant by pressing Esc a few times. The dot prompt appears.
2. Type **List** and press Enter. Your data scrolls up the screen, as shown in Figure 7.1.
3. To restrict the fields that are listed, specify the field names in the command.

   ```
   LIST LAST_NAME, FIRST_NAME, STREET
   ```

   Figure 7.2 shows a listing of the FIRST_NAME, LAST_NAME, and STREET fields from the example database.

You can include more complex commands if you're ambitious. For example, the following command lists the above three fields for

```
Record#  FIRST_NAME LAST_NAME       COMPANY                  WORK_PHONE   HOME_PHONE
   STREET                CITY            STATE ZIP
      1  Randolf    Robbins          Ralph Nicolby Inc.   415-555-1212 415-555-11
11 374 Tipplemeyer Ave.  Cornmont         CA    94709
      2  Hank       Davies           Bass-O-Matic         909-549-3787 909-398-25
63 333 33rd St.          West Goshen     SD    43312
      3  Adriator   Wegwo            Rug Flox, Inc.       321-889-3674 321-883-98
21 158 Snorewell Blvd.   Sleepyhollow    CA    02587
      4  Aretha     Phillipson       Soulariums-R-Us      908-776-5298 908-337-81
94 999 Motor City Ave.   Detroit          MI    39482
      5  Randy      Batterydown      Voltaics Inc.        809-675-4532 809-777-33
00 495 Anode St.         Carbondale      IL    30129
      6  Nimrod     Neverburger      Bab's Fish N Chips   822-991-2861 822-675-45
00 77 Easy Street        Khozad           CA    89751
      7  Marcel     Phillip          Feline Frenzy        310-563-0987 310-265-75
60 456 Fresno St.        Paris            TX    55493
      8  Valerie    Kuletski         Literary Allusions   529-221-9480 529-559-73
00 451 Farenheit Ct.     Oakland          CA    95420
      9  MARIAN     DAVIES           CITY OPERA CO.       211-334-9876 211-411-61
11 344 MARKET ST         NEW YORK         NY    10021

.
Command Line    <C:> PHONE                 Rec: EOF/9
                Enter a dBASE III PLUS command.
```

▪ ***Figure 7.1: Listing data from the dot prompt***

```
. list first_name, last_name, street
Record#  first_name last_name       street
      1  Randolf    Robbins          374 Tipplemeyer Ave.
      2  Hank       Davies           333 33rd St.
      3  Adriator   Wegwo            158 Snorewell Blvd.
      4  Aretha     Phillipson       999 Motor City Ave.
      5  Randy      Batterydown      495 Anode St.
      6  Nimrod     Neverburger      77 Easy Street
      7  Marcel     Phillip          456 Fresno St.
      8  Valerie    Kuletski         451 Farenheit Ct.
      9  MARIAN     DAVIES           344 MARKET ST

.
Command Line    <C:> PHONE                 Rec: EOF/9
                Enter a dBASE III PLUS command.
```

▪ ***Figure 7.2: Limiting the listing to selected fields***

people living in Texas *or* Illinois:

```
LIST LAST_NAME, FIRST_NAME, STREET FOR STATE
= "IL"  .OR. STATE = "TX"
```

Using quotes

Notice the quotes around the state names. The quotes are necessary when using character fields as part of a comparison. They are not required, however, when comparing numeric fields. Also notice that the fields are separated from each other by commas and spaces. Command Lines cannot break. A Command Line must not be longer than one line.

Observe the Command Line while using the Assistant to built search criteria to learn the proper syntax for entering commands at the dot prompt.

Searching Regardless of Case

The dBASE program contains many useful tools called *functions*. One such function converts data from uppercase to lowercase. Another does the reverse. These functions can be used to search out data that may have been incorrectly or inconsistently entered into your databases.

Finding Jones and JONES

In the phonebook database example shown in Figure 7.1, there are two records for Davies. One of them

```
MARIAN DAVIES
```

was accidentally entered in all caps—not an uncommon situation. A field search for Davies would not reveal this record. To avoid a problem, you can use the Upper function to find both Davies.

```
LIST FOR UPPER(LAST_NAME)="DAVIES"
```

This causes dBASE to go through all the records, look at the last name of each person, temporarily convert it to uppercase, and check to see if it equals "DAVIES."

Finding Embedded Strings

Suppose you want to search for a word in the middle of a field—part of a street address or company name, for example. Such a word is called an *embedded string*. A *string* is any series of letters or numbers in a character field and is called embedded if it's surrounded by other words or characters.

The dBASE program uses the dollar ($) sign, called the *substring search function,* to find embedded strings. If you wanted to search for the record of anyone living on Snorewell Blvd., you would enter

```
LIST FOR "Snorewell" $STREET
```

Translated, this command means "Display the first name, last name, and street address fields of any record where the street address has the word *Snorewell* embedded in it." Type in the character string you're searching for, making sure you place quotes around it, followed by a dollar sign and the name of the field you want searched.

Organizing Records for Faster Access

The ordering of records in even small databases is often haphazard. Typically, records are added to databases as they become available, and thus are stored in a more or less random order. However, there are times when it is useful to arrange an entire database to suit a specific purpose. This Step explains how to easily arrange records in a variety of ways.

AN OVERVIEW OF ORDERING TECHNIQUES

A telephone book is a good example of a database that has been arranged after the fact. Once the telephone company has collected all the names it's going to publish, it then organizes them according to last name so that you can easily look someone up.

Sorting and indexing

There are two ways to achieve this type of ordering with dBASE: *sorting* and *indexing*. Sorting actually rearranges the records and writes the newly ordered database on disk. By contrast, indexing doesn't change the original order of the records. Instead, it simulates a sorted database by using an *index file*, explained below.

When it comes to arranging records, indexing is generally the preferred technique. This is because it makes it easier to update your databases. Indexed databases re-sort themselves automatically as you edit your data. You don't have to worry about it. Sorted databases, however, have to be manually re-sorted.

When to sort

There are times, though, when you'll want to sort. In fact, it may be your only option when you want to transfer your database to another database program or to a computer that doesn't use dBASE index files.

SORTING A DATABASE

Consider the small database shown in Figure 8.1, a camping trip inventory. To reorder the records by weight, you'd complete the following steps:

1. Select Organize/Sort.
2. A field list appears. Choose the field you want to base the sort on (in this case, WEIGHT)—this is called the *key field.* Highlight it and press Enter, then press → to leave the field list.

   Key field
3. Since the file is actually rearranged and written to disk, you get to choose a file name and disk drive location for

```
. list
Record#  ITEM        WEIGHT  COST OWNER
      1  Back pack       10 65.00 Rich
      2  Stove           25 85.00 Rich
      3  Tent            12 62.33 Lisa B.
      4  Food            30 45.27 Group
      5  Rain Gear        7 12.95 Renee
      6  Flashlight       2  7.50 Jean
      7  Hammock          5 15.00 John

.
.
.
.
Command Line    ||<C:>||CAMPING              ||Rec: EOF/7          ||    ||

                         Enter a dBASE III PLUS command.
```

■ *Figure 8.1: A small database of camping gear*

the sorted file. Type in a name and press Enter. The file is sorted and stored on disk.

4. To see the results of your sort, open the newly created file (in this example, CAMP2) and list the contents. The results are shown in Figure 8.2

Notice that the list in Figure 8.2 is organized in ascending order by weight. By default dBASE assumes this order. If you want to sort in descending order, you must work from the dot prompt.

Ascending versus descending order

1. Turn off the Assistant and go to the dot prompt.
2. Add the word *DESCENDING* to the normal Sort command. Here's an example that would sort the camping list by descending weight:

```
SORT ON WEIGHT TO CAMP3 DESCENDING
```

CAMP3 is the newly sorted file's name.

I already mentioned that you must re-sort the database when you add new records or edit the key field of existing records. For small databases, that's not much hassle. For large databases, though, this can take a lot of time and disk space. Each sorted copy of the

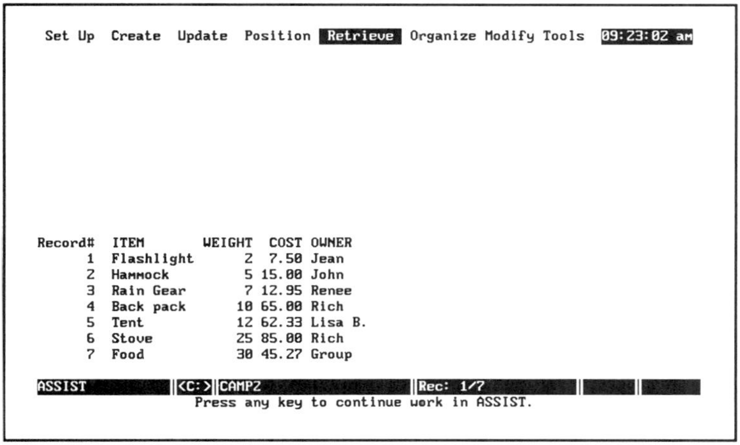

■ *Figure 8.2: The camping list, sorted by weight*

database is as large as the original database, and you'll create a copy each time you sort the database and store it under a new file name. If you do decide to maintain several copies of a database, be sure to make your changes to only one, which you've designated the master list. Then re-sort that one.

INDEXING A DATABASE

Indexing avoids all the problems associated with sorting and has other advantages, besides. Instead of rewriting the sorted data on disk as a completely new database file, indexing uses a separate, smaller *pointer file* to order the records in the main database. This works in much the same way a card catalogue in a library does. Instead of searching through all the books in a library, you look through card indexes (author, subject, and title) to point you to the actual book you want.

Indexing offers another benefit. Indexed databases allow you to use the Seek command, which is very similar, though significantly faster, than Locate. It lets you find a desired record quickly.

How to Create the Index

Creating an index is similar to sorting.

1. Make sure your database file is open.
2. Choose Organize/Index. A box appears asking for information (see Figure 8.3).
3. You can type in the name of the field on which you want the index based, or press F10 for a field list, from which you can select the key field.
4. Press Enter. Just as with sorting, you need to specify where the index (pointer) file is to be stored and what its name is. You should store it on the same disk as the database file. Choose the drive and press Enter. Now choose the file name—it's easiest just to use the key field name. Then press Enter.

5. In a few seconds the file is indexed. You can simply list the file to see the new order—you don't have to open another file as you did after sorting. Figure 8.4 shows an example of an indexed file.

Notice that the record numbers (along the left margin) are now out of order even though the records themselves appear in order by increasing weight. As with the library example, the books (here, record numbers) remain in their original order on the shelf, though the pointers have been rearranged.

You can create as many indexes as you want, switching them on or off for the purposes of retrieving data in a variety of orders. As soon as you create a new index, dBASE activates it.

Multiple indexes

Activating an Index

Master index

The index that is currently in use is called the Master index. Other indexes may be open so that they are automatically updated as you add or edit records, but only the Master index controls the order of the listings. Obviously you'll have to switch to a different Master index

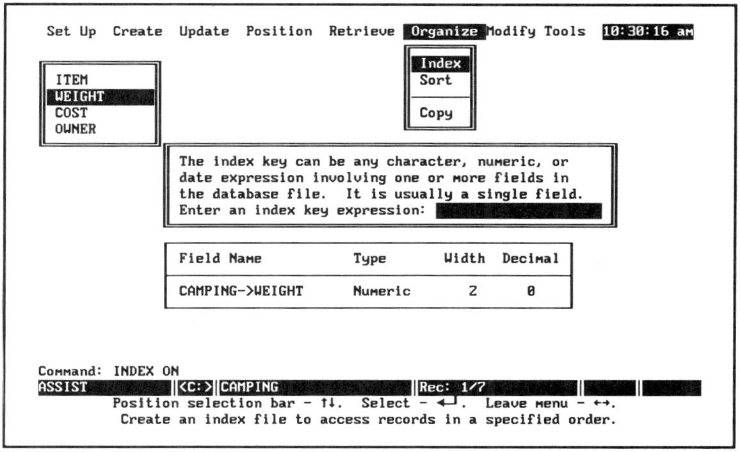

■ *Figure 8.3: Creating a new index*

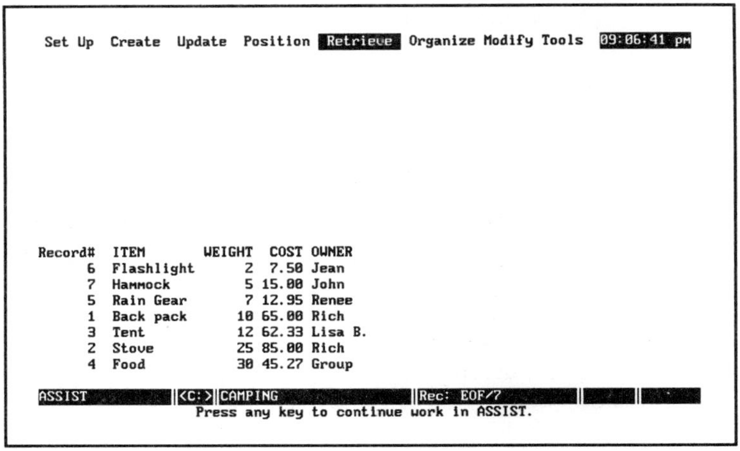

▪ ***Figure 8.4: The camping list after indexing by weight***

if you want to change the apparent order of records. To designate a Master, follow these steps:

1. Choose Setup/Database file.
2. Select the drive and database name.
3. When asked if the file is indexed, answer **Yes.**
4. Choose the index(es) you want to activate. The first one you choose becomes the Master index and gets the word *Master* written in after it. Subsequent indexes will be numbered 2, 3, 4, and so on (these are called secondary indexes). You may have as many as seven indexes active at one time. All will be automatically updated as you add, delete, and edit your records.

Automatic updating

Seeing Active Indexes

Things can get confusing when you have a number of indexes. After switching between them, you may forget which one is the Master index and which others are active. To keep track of what's going on, follow these steps:

1. Go to the dot prompt.
2. Type **Display Status** and press Enter. A list of information appears on the screen, including the names of open indexes.

Using Seek to Find Records FAST!

The main reason for indexing is so that you can use the Seek command. Seek lets you locate a desired record quickly, whereas listing out an entire database or using the Locate command can take ages. The only thing you have to remember is that Seek must be used with the key field and works only with the Master index.

Say we want to quickly find out what a $7.50 camping trip receipt was for.

1. Create an index based on the COST field. Activate it.
2. From the Assistant, select Position/Seek.
3. A box appears asking you to enter an *expression*. The Message Line reads

   `Enter a constant for comparison`

   This is dBASE jargon for "What do you want to look for?" In this case, you type in **7.50** and press Enter.
4. Though it appears nothing has happened, dBASE went looking for the record where the cost was $7.50 and positioned the record pointer on it. To see the record, select Retrieve/Display/Execute the Command.

If Seek can't find the item you're looking for, you'll get the message

`No find`

just above the Status Line. You might also get this message if you have the wrong index open. If no index is open, you won't be able to select the Seek command.

Seek with character fields

The example above used a Numeric field, so $7.50 can be entered without quotes. If you are seeking data that is stored in a Character field (such as a name or address), you'll have to put quotes on each side of the expression (e.g., "Rich"). If you forget the quotes, you'll see the message

```
Variable not found
```

Updating large databases

The more indexes you have open, the slower things get, especially when you are adding records to your database. This is because dBASE has to update all the active indexes to include each record added. Try to keep the number of indexes to a minimum, unless your database is going to remain small.

Updating Your Records

There will undoubtedly be a time when you'll want to alter a record in your database. The dBASE program allows you to edit your data records easily. In this Step, you'll learn several techniques for updating your records and eliminating unwanted records from a database.

If your file is indexed, be sure the indexes are open when you make the changes. If you intend to find the records you want to edit by using Seek, also make sure you have the correct Master index selected.

MODIFYING DATA WITH EDIT

The most straightforward way to change data in a record is to use the *Edit* command. This is an option from the Update menu that works in much the same way as Append. One record is displayed at a time and you can move the cursor around to make your changes.

1. First open the database containing the record you want to edit.
2. Use either the Seek or Locate command to move the record pointer to the record you want to work with.

3. Choose Update/Edit. The record appears on the screen (see Figure 9.1). The display looks similar to that for a record in the Append mode, but the Status Line indicates you're in the Edit mode.

Moving between records and fields

You can move between records using the PgUp and PgDn keys. PgUp moves to the previous record, PgDn moves to the next record. If you prefer, you can also use Ctrl-R to move to the previous record, or Ctrl-C to move to the next record.

Move the highlight between fields using the Enter key or the arrow keys. When you get to the last field of a record, press Enter to jump to the next record (if you're on the last record, pressing Enter takes you back to the Assistant).

Editing keys

To make changes to the data in a record, use the editing keys shown in the Help box at the top of the screen. If the box isn't available, press F1 to display it. The alternative Ctrl-key codes are listed in Step 5.

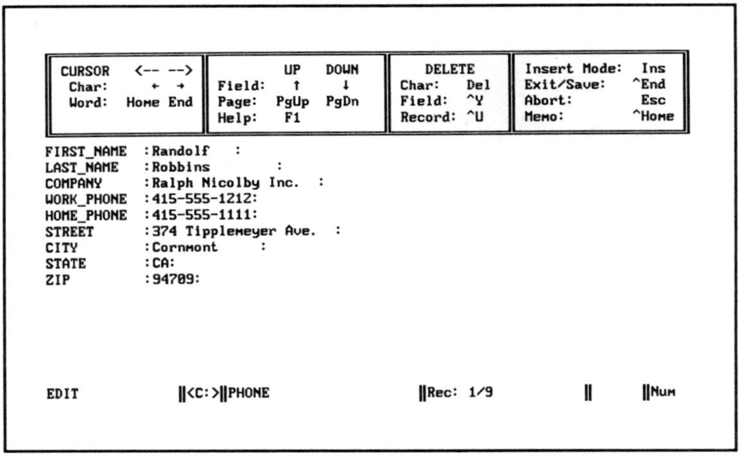

■ *Figure 9.1: Using Edit is similar to using Append*

See Step 15 for information about editing Memo fields.

MODIFYING DATA WITH BROWSE

There is another dBASE option that can make updating your database a bit easier, particularly if you plan on editing more than a few records. *Browse* lets you scan through your database by rows and columns. Using keyboard commands, you can scroll left, right, up, and down to see all the fields and records, editing as you go. You can also add or delete records in this mode.

Browse will display as many records as will fit on the screen, with one record per line. The fields that don't fit on the screen extend beyond its edge. The column of record numbers you normally see when listing data is not shown when you are in the Browse mode, however.

1. Make sure you've opened a database file and activated any indexes you want.
2. Move the record pointer to the top of the file by selecting Position/Goto Record/Top. This causes Browse to begin its display with the first record. (If you have an index active, this probably isn't the *true* first record—remember that though indexing changes the apparent order of records, it does not affect their actual positions. Thus, the first record shown may be only the first record according to the indexing order.)
3. Choose Update/Browse. Figure 9.2 shows an example of a small database in the Browse mode. Note that the column headings are actually the field names.

Editing in the Browse Mode

If you don't see the editing keys while browsing, press F1 to display them. Table 9.1 summarizes the Browse mode keyboard commands.

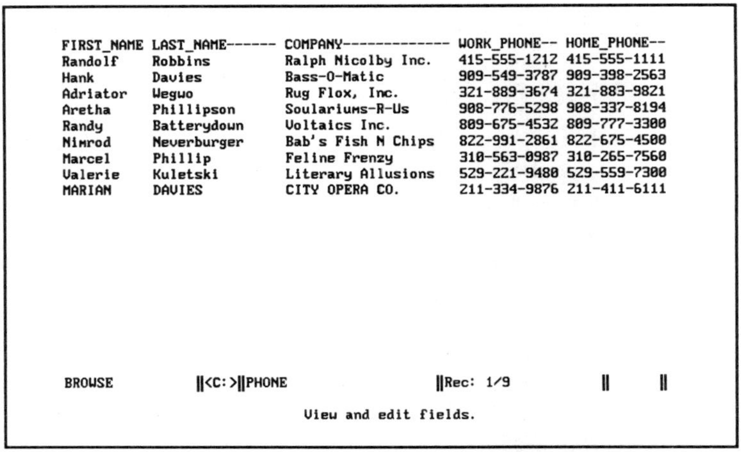

```
FIRST_NAME LAST_NAME------ COMPANY------------- WORK_PHONE-- HOME_PHONE--
Randolf    Robbins         Ralph Nicolby Inc.   415-555-1212 415-555-1111
Hank       Davies          Bass-O-Matic         909-549-3787 909-398-2563
Adriator   Wegwo           Rug Flox, Inc.       321-889-3674 321-883-9821
Aretha     Phillipson      Solariums-R-Us       908-776-5298 908-337-8194
Randy      Batterydown     Voltaics Inc.        809-675-4532 809-777-3300
Nimrod     Neverburger     Bab's Fish N Chips   822-991-2861 822-675-4500
Marcel     Phillip         Feline Frenzy        310-563-0987 310-265-7560
Valerie    Kuletski        Literary Allusions   529-221-9480 529-559-7300
MARIAN     DAVIES          CITY OPERA CO.       211-334-9876 211-411-6111

BROWSE          ||<C:>||PHONE            ||Rec: 1/9        ||     ||
                       View and edit fields.
```

■ ***Figure 9.2: Record viewing and editing can be done in Browse mode***

Main Key	*Letter Key*	*Action*
Home	^A	Move left one field
End	^F	Move right one field
←	^S	Move left one letter
→	^D	Move right one letter
↑	^E	Save record and move up one record
↓	^X	Save record and move down one record
	^R	Save record and move up one screen
→	^B	Pan screen to the right
←	^Z	Pan screen to the left
Del	^G	Delete character at cursor position
	^Y	Delete from cursor to end of field

Main Key	Letter Key	Action
	^U	Mark entire record for later deletion
^End	^W	Save changes in current record and exit Browse
Esc	^Q	Forget changes in current record and exit Browse

Table 9.1: Editing keys for Browse mode

When editing a record in Browse, just moving to another record causes any changes you made to be saved. Thus, pressing Ctrl-Q to abandon changes only affects the record you are currently working on. In other words, if you mess up several records and then type Ctrl-Q, only the last record will be spared—you won't be able to prevent the other records from being altered.

Memo Fields

Note that you can't edit or display Memo text fields from the Browse mode. See Step 15 for a complete discussion of Memo fields.

Panning

If your database contains more than a few fields, you probably won't be able to see all the fields at once. To bring the fields into view, you'll need to *pan* left and right.

1. Press Ctrl→ and the display will scroll one field to the left. That is, the first field will scroll off the left side of the screen and a new field will appear on the right. Press again to repeat the process.
2. Press Ctrl← to move the display one field to the right.

Adding Records

You can add records in the Browse mode, too.

1. Move to the last record using the arrow keys or other navigation keys.
2. Press ↓. The Message Line reads

```
Add new records? (Y/N)
```

3. Type **Y**. New, blank fields appear ready for data entry. Just press Enter at this point if you want to quit the appending process.

Other Browse Options

Saving Time

There are other Browse options that make it easier to move around and see particular fields. While in the Browse mode, pressing F10 causes six menu selections to appear at the top of the screen. Here's what each one does:

Bottom Moves the cursor to the last record (bottom) of the database. Simply highlight the option and press Enter, or type **B**.

Top Moves the cursor to the first record (top) of the database. Highlight the option and press Enter, or type **T**.

Lock Lets you specify fields to remain stationary on the screen, even during panning. (Specify first the leftmost field you want locked.) See the section below to learn more about the Lock option.

Record no. Gets you to any record number quickly. When prompted, supply the number of the record you want to see.

Freeze Lets you specify one particular field to edit. All other fields are displayed but cannot be modified. Instructions for using the command are given below.

Find This command appears only if the file is indexed and an index is active. It quickly finds the record matching data you input. The Find command is described more fully below.

Locking fields

Sometimes you'll want to keep specific fields containing identifying data on screen while panning. For example, in Figure 9.2, it might be useful to keep the FIRST_NAME and LAST_NAME fields on the screen so that the data in the STREET field can be conveniently and accurately edited (see Figure 9.3).

The process of locking fields must always begin with the leftmost field you want locked. From there, any number of adjacent fields to the right can also be locked.

```
FIRST_NAME LAST_NAME------ STREET---------------- CITY--------- STATE ZIP--
Randolf    Robbins         374 Tipplemeyer Ave.   Cornmont      CA    94709
Hank       Davies          333 33rd St.           West Goshen   SD    43312
Adriator   Weguo           158 Snorewell Blvd.    Sleepyhollow  CA    02587
Aretha     Phillipson      999 Motor City Ave.    Detroit       MI    39482
Randy      Batterydown     495 Anode St.          Carbondale    IL    30129
Nimrod     Neverburger     77 Easy Street         Khozad        CA    89751
Marcel     Phillip         456 Fresno St.         Paris         TX    55493
Valerie    Kuletski        451 Farenheit Ct.      Oakland       CA    95420
MARIAN     DAVIES          344 MARKET ST          NEW YORK      NY    10021







BROWSE          ||<C:>||PHONE              ||Rec: 1/9        ||      ||
                          View and edit fields.
```

▪ ***Figure 9.3: The FIRST_NAME and LAST_NAME fields***

1. Pan right or left so that the leftmost field you want to lock is at the left edge of the screen.
2. Press F10 and select Lock by highlighting it and pressing Enter.
3. You'll be asked for the number of columns to lock. Type in the desired number and press Enter. (Two fields are locked in Figure 9.3.)

Unlocking fields

To unlock fields, choose the Lock command again and just press Enter without typing a number.

Freezing fields

To edit only one field while browsing, use the Freeze command. This way, other fields won't be altered accidentally and you won't have to keep jumping between fields or searching for the cursor.

1. Press F10.
2. Choose Freeze.
3. Type in the name of the field you want to freeze and press Enter.

To unfreeze a field, choose the Freeze command again, do not specify a field name, and press Enter.

Using the Find command

If your file is indexed and if the index is active, you can quickly jump to any record by following these steps.

1. Press F10.
2. Choose Find. (The quickest way is to press ← once, then Enter.)
3. The program prompts you:

   ```
   Enter search string:
   ```

   Type in the information you want to match. Remember that it must be in the key field of the record you want to locate (you don't have to use quotes, though). Now press Enter.

If a record matching the search can't be found, dBASE responds with

```
** Not Found **
```

DELETING UNWANTED RECORDS

In addition to editing, you'll probably want to cull unwanted records from your databases once in a while. Keeping your database clean and uncluttered is crucial to the efficiency of dBASE III PLUS. Duplicate, incomplete, erroneous, and outdated records can slow down many dBASE processes. They can also lead to other types of data contamination, so it is good practice to regularly purge your database of unwanted records.

Marking Individual Records for Deletion

Pressing Ctrl-U when you are in the Edit or Browse mode marks the current record for later deletion. The word *Del* appears on the Status Line when you do this and the Delete option inserts a code that is used later for eliminating the record. Pressing Ctrl-U doesn't actually erase the record from the database, to protect you against accidents. Pressing Ctrl-U a second time removes the message.

Marking Multiple Records for Deletion

You can mark a series of records for deletion by building a search condition or specifying a scope. You can use this approach to eliminate all records of people who haven't purchased an item from your store in over a year, for example, or eliminate inventory records of a specific type.

1. Choose Update/Delete/Build a Search Condition (or Specify Scope).
2. Set up the search condition. (Refer to Step 7 if you need to refresh your memory).
3. Execute the command.

All records matching the specification will be marked for deletion. The number of deletions is reported on the Command Line.

Unmarking Records

If you decide that you really want to keep some or all of your marked records after all, you can unmark, or *recall,* them. Recalling has the same effect as moving to a marked record while in the Browse or Edit mode and pressing Ctrl-U. To use the Recall command, follow these steps.

1. Choose Update/Recall.
2. Executing the command at this point will unmark the current record. If you want to recall a whole group of records, set up a scope or search condition. To recall *all* marked records, select All from the Scope box.
3. Execute the command.

The Command Line tells you how many records were recalled.

Using the Packing Command

The process of actually deleting marked records is called *packing.* Simply choose the Pack command from the Update menu—there are no option boxes to choose from with this command.

This is a powerful command. One false move and your marked records will vanish irretrievably.

If your database is indexed, make sure the indexes are active when you issue the Pack command. The program will then automatically update the indexes for you, reflecting any changes made to the data base. If you forget to do this, recreate the indexes as explained in Step 8.

A good technique for determining which records to delete is to print out your database on paper. Use the List option from the Assistant and send the listing to the printer. Mark up the paper, then return to the computer to make the changes.

30

Creating Reports

Now that you know how to enter, retrieve, edit, and maintain your data, you're ready to learn how to create reports. Unlike simple listing, reporting lets you fine-tune the printed page for a finished, professional look. Reports can include not only data, but also headers and footers, as well as calculated subtotals, totals, and summaries. If you choose, you can print only certain fields. You can also replace cryptic field names with comprehensible column headings.

The Report Form generator

The *Report Form generator* built into dBASE III PLUS can create fairly sophisticated printouts of your database information within minutes. Even though this feature is not advanced enough to create highly complex reports, it can produce everyday documents such as a general ledger, a list of sales figures for the year, mailing labels, or an inventory list.

The examples in this and several subsequent Steps draw on a small database of inventory for a stereo store. Figure 10.1 lists the database.

```
Set Up  Create  Update  Position  Retrieve  Organize  Modify  Tools  06:19:10 pm

Record#  CATEGORY    BRAND       MODEL   QUANTITY WHOLESALE RETAIL
      1  RECEIVER    NIZO        T-33    5           225.49 350.49
      2  RECEIVER    NIZO        T-35    4           312.00 425.25
      3  RECEIVER    ACME        RZ5-MT  13           19.99  49.99
      4  RECEIVER    NADIR       Z-CHP   50           12.95  29.99
      5  SPEAKERS    RAZCO       L-55    30          199.00 249.00
      6  SPEAKERS    TALBEST     BG-20   6           250.00 350.88
      7  TAPE DECK   ROLLEM      CAS-3   10          125.65 212.99
      8  TAPE DECK   FLOWUTTER   WBL-5   5           149.33 250.77
      9  TURNTABLE   XIRTAM      25-L    5            99.99 149.99
     10  TURNTABLE   RALURIC     RND-1   3           595.00 850.00

ASSIST          ||<C:>||STEREO              ||Rec: 1/10          ||      ||   Caps
                Press any key to continue work in ASSIST.
```

■ ***Figure 10.1: The STEREO database***

DESIGNING THE REPORT

Suppose you want to create a simple report from the information in our sample database that does the following:

- Lists all the products in inventory.
- Calculates the total investment (wholesale cost) tied up in the inventory.
- Calculates the total investment for each type of item (receivers, speakers, etc.).
- Calculates the percentage gross margin for each item, based on the price markup from wholesale to retail.

A report that accomplishes all of this is shown in Figure 10.2. Adapt the steps below to create a report from any database.

1. Open the database.
2. From the Assistant, choose Create/Report.
3. Select the drive designator.
4. Name the report **STEREO**. The program automatically

Page No. 1
06/25/91

Uncle Bob's HiFi Inventory

Brand	Category	Model	Quan.	My Cost	Retail	Invested	Margin
NIZO	RECEIVER	T-33	7	225.49	350.49	1578.43	35.66
NIZO	RECEIVER	T-35	4	312.00	425.25	1248.00	26.63
ACME	RECEIVER	R25-MT	15	19.99	49.99	299.85	60.01
NADIR	RECEIVER	2-CHP	50	12.95	29.99	647.50	56.82
RAZCO	SPEAKERS	L-55	31	199.00	249.00	6169.00	20.08
TALBEST	SPEAKERS	BG-20	7	250.00	350.88	1750.00	28.75
ROLLEM	TAPE DECK	CAS-3	11	125.65	212.99	1382.15	41.01
FLOWUTTER	TAPE DECK	WBL-5	5	149.33	250.77	746.65	40.45
BLABBEX	TELEVISION	K22	29	189.99	249.99	5509.71	24.00
BIG-VUE	TELEVISION	BV-45	6	595.00	750.00	3570.00	20.67
XIRTAM	TURNTABLE	25-L	5	99.99	149.99	499.95	33.34
RALURIC	TURNTABLE	RND-1	3	595.00	850.00	1785.00	30.00
CINOSANAP	VCR	TP-120	3	540.99	345.89	1622.97	-56.41
THINEX	VCR	TV-29	14	149.00	199.00	2086.00	25.13
MAXWELL	VIDEO TAPE	XX-120	45	3.49	4.99	157.05	30.06
*** Total ***							
			235			29052.26	

■ ***Figure 10.2: The finished report***

adds an *.FRM* extension to the name—do not enter an extension yourself.

5. The Report screen appears with the Options menu open. Highlight the Columns menu. A blank report form appears at the bottom of the page.

A basic report

6. To create the report, first set up your options. These include report title, single or double spacing, and so forth.
7. Decide if records should be subgrouped for visual impact or for calculating subtotals (subtotaling is covered later in this Step). Select what data will appear in each column of the report and assign each a column title. If the column is numerical, indicate whether it should be totaled at the bottom.
8. Save the report file.

Assigning the page title

9. Select Options\Page Title. In the box, type in the page title that will appear at the top of each page of your report. Press Ctrl-End. The first few words of the heading appear in the Options box.

10. You can change any of the other settings on the Options menu, such as line spacing and margins, if you like. Highlight an option for a Help Line explanation of its function.

Setting Up the Columns

Column widths

You can make a column any size you like. However, there are a few considerations to keep in mind. While Character fields will wrap around within a column, allowing you some flexibility, the same is not true for Numeric fields. Allowing extra space for each column will separate them on the page. Experiment to find the optimum column widths.

To set up the columns for the report, follow the steps below.

1. Choose Columns/Contents. A box containing five items appears. The first item (Contents) is highlighted and an arrow waits for you to indicate which field's information you want listed in the first column of your report.
2. You have two options for responding. You can type in a field name, or press F10 to see a Field list and pick a field from it. It's wisest to press F10—now you can see how long each field is, which is helpful when you format the report. For the stereo store report, I chose the BRAND field for column 1.
3. Normally, you'll want to show just the contents of the field in the column. If this is what you want, simply press Enter again. However, keep in mind that you can construct more elaborate columns by stuffing the data from several fields into one column. You can even instruct dBASE to place the results of a calculation there.
4. Move down to the next line, Heading, by pressing ↓ and Enter. A small box appears. Type in the heading you want at the top of column 1, and press Ctrl-End to save the heading. I've entered *Brand.*

Increasing space between columns

5. Set the width for the column by highlighting Width and pressing Enter. The column width and decimal places are

assumed by dBASE to be the size of the field or the size of the column heading, whichever is greater. You can type over this setting if you want. Increasing it will add space between your columns.

6. Set the decimal places, if necessary, by highlighting Decimal and pressing Enter. Type over the default and press Enter again.

Numeric field totals

7. Next, indicate whether you want the column totaled at the bottom. In our example, BRAND is a Character field, so it's irrelevant. Keep in mind, however, that dBASE will assume that you want all Numeric fields totaled. If you *don't* want a total at the bottom of a Numeric column, highlight

   `Total this column`

   and press Enter to change the setting to No. Press Enter to toggle between Yes and No.

Saving your work

8. Press PgDn to save the first column's definition and move to the next one. Our report form now looks like Figure 10.3. (The large box at the bottom of the screen is sort of a

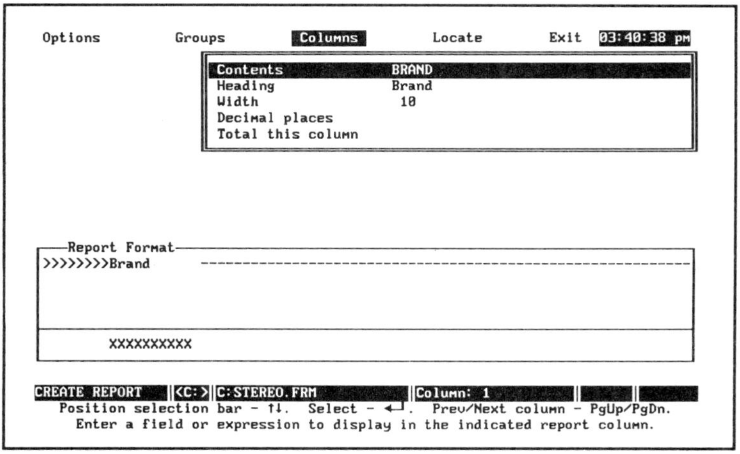

■ ***Figure 10.3: The first column of the report defined***

compressed version of the final printed page, indicating what's going to be in each column.)

9. Define the rest of your columns, repeating the above steps. Remember to highlight the item you're setting and press Enter before entering your information. Also, remember to press Ctrl-End to save each heading and then PgDn to skip ahead to the next field.

Adding Calculated Fields

As I mentioned above, normally you print just the contents of fields in the columns. However, you can have dBASE do calculations "on the fly" for you as it prints reports. Calculations can be based on data in one or more fields. In our example, dBASE will calculate and print the total investment for each item (quantity multiplied by wholesale cost). The asterisk (*) indicates multiplication, so the contents of column 7 as you see it in the report is the result of

```
QUANTITY*WHOLESALE
```

The last column has a somewhat more complex formula for its contents:

```
((Retail-Wholesale)/Retail)*100
```

The result displayed is the percentage gross margin for each item (i.e., the markup as a percentage of the retail price). Note how the parentheses have to be used carefully, just as they are in algebra. The pair around Retail - Wholesale tells dBASE to calculate the subtraction first, then the division. Finally, the multiplication is calculated.

Saving the Form

Figure 10.4 shows the sample report screen with all eight columns in place. Notice each column's heading and the representation of the data location below that.

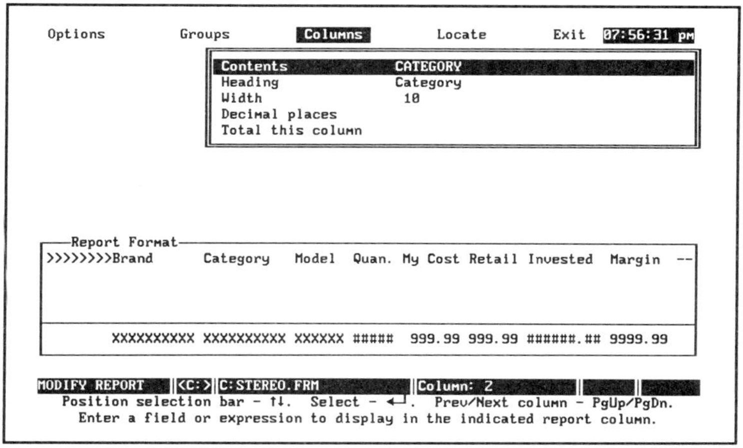

▪ ***Figure 10.4: The report form, ready to go***

To save the form, follow these steps:

1. Save the last column with Ctrl-End, if necessary.
2. Press **E** to open the Exit menu.
3. Choose Save.

You're returned to the Assistant or dot prompt (depending on where you started). Now you can run the report.

VIEWING AND PRINTING THE REPORT

To see the fruits of your labor, do one of the following:

- From the Assistant, select Retrieve/Report. Select the drive and the form by name, just as when opening a database file. Execute the command. If you want the report printed, answer **Y** to the question about the printer. To view it on the screen, press **N**.
- From the dot prompt, use the Report Form command followed by the name of the report:

  ```
  REPORT FORM STEREO
  ```

and press Enter. This command sends the report to the screen for viewing. To print the report, type

```
REPORT FORM STEREO TO PRINT
```

- Press Enter. The result is shown in Figure 10.2.

This might seem like a lot of work for a simple listing, but for a large database, or one that changes often, it's worth the time. You can run the report as often as necessary simply by selecting it from the file list.

Modifying the Report to Add Subtotals

Just as with database structures and data, you can modify a report form after the fact to incorporate changes you think of later. Thus, your reports can evolve over time.

The trick to preparing a good report is to ask the right questions, then create a report that can answer them. Subtotaling helps to accomplish this. The process groups records by a common element and subtotals the data in selected fields.

Subtotaling

With the stereo store inventory, I wanted to group each type of equipment (receivers, tape decks, etc.) and subtotal each group (see Figure 10.5).

Creating groups

The most important part of subtotaling is creating the groups of records on which each subtotal is based. Ask yourself, "What do the records I want to group have in common?" That is, which field has identical data for each record in the group? In our example, CATEGORY is the common field—that's the field that identifies the item type (receiver, tape deck, speaker, and so on). The program can group the records that have the word *receiver* in them, for example, and produce the subtotal.

To modify the STEREO.FRM report file to include subtotals for each category, follow the steps below. (Of course, you can use the

```
Page No.      1
06/25/91
                         Uncle Bob's HiFi Inventory

Brand       Category    Model   Quan. My Cost Retail   Invested   Margin


** Figures for all RECEIVER
 NIZO       RECEIVER    T-33       7  225.49 350.49    1578.43    35.66
 NIZO       RECEIVER    T-35       4  312.00 425.25    1248.00    26.63
 ACME       RECEIVER    R25-MT    15   19.99  49.99     299.85    60.01
 NADIR      RECEIVER    2-CHP     50   12.95  29.99     647.50    56.82
** Subtotal **
                                  76                   3773.78

** Figures for all SPEAKERS
 RAZCO      SPEAKERS    L-55      31  199.00 249.00    6169.00    20.08
 TALBEST    SPEAKERS    BG-20      7  250.00 350.88    1750.00    28.75
** Subtotal **
                                  38                   7919.00

** Figures for all TAPE DECK
 ROLLEM     TAPE DECK   CAS-3     11  125.65 212.99    1382.15    41.01
 FLOWUTTER  TAPE DECK   WBL-5      5  149.33 250.77     746.65    40.45
** Subtotal **
                                  16                   2128.80

** Figures for all TELEVISION
 BLABBEX    TELEVISION K22        29  189.99 249.99    5509.71    24.00
 BIG-VUE    TELEVISION BV-45       6  595.00 750.00    3570.00    20.67
** Subtotal **
                                  35                   9079.71

** Figures for all TURNTABLE
 XIRTAM     TURNTABLE   25-L       5   99.99 149.99     499.95    33.34
 RALURIC    TURNTABLE   RND-1      3  595.00 850.00    1785.00    30.00
** Subtotal **
                                   8                   2284.95

** Figures for all VCR
 CINOSANAP  VCR         TP-120     3  540.99 345.89    1622.97   -56.41
 THINEX     VCR         TV-29     14  149.00 199.00    2086.00    25.13
** Subtotal **
                                  17                   3708.97

** Figures for all VIDEO TAPE
 MAXWELL    VIDEO TAPE XX-120     45    3.49   4.99     157.05    30.06
** Subtotal **
                                  45                    157.05
*** Total ***
                                 235                  29052.26
```

▪ ***Figure 10.5: Subtotals added to the report***

same basic procedure when initially creating a report, too. Begin with step 3.)

1. From the Assistant, select Modify/Report.
2. Select the drive letter and the report name, STEREO.FRM.
3. When the Report screen comes up, highlight Groups/Group on Expression, and press Enter. The little arrow appears.

STEP 10

4. Type in the name of the field on which the grouping is based. In this case, type **CATEGORY**. As an alternative, you could press F10 and choose from a Field list.

Note that when you want to include subtotals in a report, the file must either be indexed or sorted by the field on which the grouping is based. Otherwise, your subtotals will be a mess. Instead of all the items in a particular class being grouped together, the individual records will be scattered throughout the report. (The STEREO database was sorted by the CATEGORY field.)

5. Press ↓ once to move down to Group Heading, and press Enter. Now you type in the heading you want to appear before each grouping. In the example, I entered *Figures for All* (see Figure 10.4). Notice how dBASE filled in the category after each heading (i.e., Figures for All RECEIVER).

6. Save the report and run it.

OPTIONS FOR YOUR REPORTS

Some options to consider while designing your reports are listed below.

- Under the Groups settings there is an option for Summary Report Only. If you set this option to Yes, the details of each category are eliminated and only the subtotals remain.
- The Page Eject After Group option will print a separate page for each category.
- The Locate menu takes you directly to a selected column. This prevents having to use the PgUp and PgDn keys repeatedly while making modifications under the Column menu.
- When not subtotaling, you can index or sort on any field for the purpose of the report. For example, if you want records listed by brand, index on the BRAND field, activate the index, then run the report.

- Finally, don't overlook the Build a Search Condition option when running a report from the Assistant. This option works the same way with reports as it does with List or Display. For example, say you want to see only the totals for turntables, or for products from ACME. Just build the condition in the usual way, then run the report.

15

Generating Mailing Labels

In Step 10 you learned how to create standard reports. This Step introduces a slightly different type of report—mailing labels. You probably don't think of mailing labels as reports, but remember that the computer is simply printing your data in a predefined format, as before.

Printing labels is one of the classic examples of how your computer can save you time. The *Label generator* built into dBASE III PLUS makes it easy to print addresses neatly on various sizes of commercially available pressure-sensitive labels.

Printer requirements

If you're using wide label stock, you can print as many as four labels across the page. Since spacing and alignment are critical, you need a printer with a tractor feeder or a laser printer to feed the labels accurately.

For this Step, I'll create two-column mailing labels using the phonebook database example, PHONE. You can easily apply the techniques to your own databases.

STEP 11

PREPARING THE LABEL DATA

Since the U.S. Post Office requires bulk mailings to be in zip code order, you'll want to index your database before printing. (The Post Office does not require you to sort First Class mailings, however.)

As when creating a report, you have to design a form. The program uses the form as a template for each label it prints. Design the label form using the Label screen.

1. Open the PHONE database.
2. Index or sort it by zip code, if necessary.
3. Choose Create/Label, select the drive, and give the file a name. The program automatically adds the *.LBL* extension. The Label screen appears, as you see in Figure 11.1.

The Options menu

There are only two menus you have to deal with here—Options and Contents. Options lets you select from five different predefined label formats. If none of these suits your needs, you can modify the label specifications. The six modifications possible are explained in Table 11.1. The five predefined sizes work for most popular label types, however.

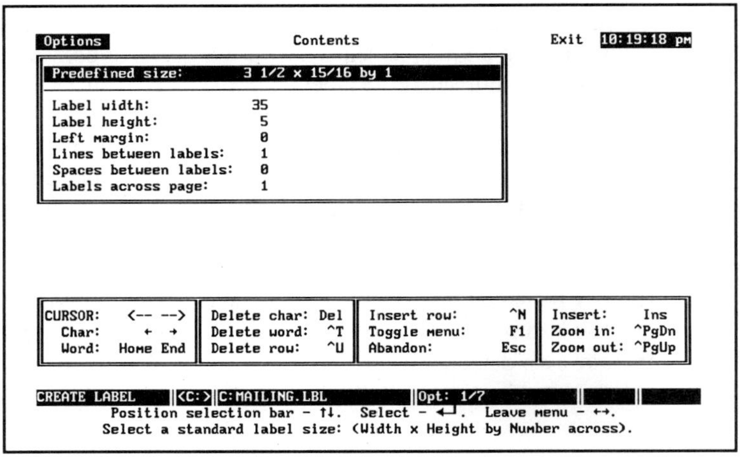

▪ ***Figure 11.1: The Label screen***

Option	*Meaning*
Label width	Number of characters on any one line of the label. Maximum is 20.
Label height	Number of lines on one label. Select from 1 to 16.
Left margin	Number of spaces from the left edge of the backing paper to the first printed letter. Select from 0 to 250.
Lines between labels	Vertical distance, in blank lines, between two labels. Select from 0 to 16.
Spaces between labels	Horizontal distance, in spaces, between two labels. Select from 0 to 120.
Labels across page	Number of labels to be printed across the page. Select from 1 to 15.

Table 11.1: Available label format modifications

1. Highlight the first line in the Options menu and press Enter a few times. Notice that each time you press Enter, the label size changes, as do the other settings in the box. For this example, use the setting

   ```
   3 1/2 x 15/16 by 2
   ```

   "By 2" specifies that you want to print two labels across the page.

3. Check Table 11.1 to see if you want to alter any other settings in the Options box. In most cases, you won't need to adjust anything.

The Contents menu

4. Press → to open the Contents menu. Each numbered line represents a line on the label, from top to bottom. Press Enter on line 1.

5. The little arrow appears. You can now press F10 to bring up a Field list, or type in the field names. Press Enter after entering the information on each line, then press ↓ to advance to the next line. Figure 11.2 shows the completed form for our phonebook database example.

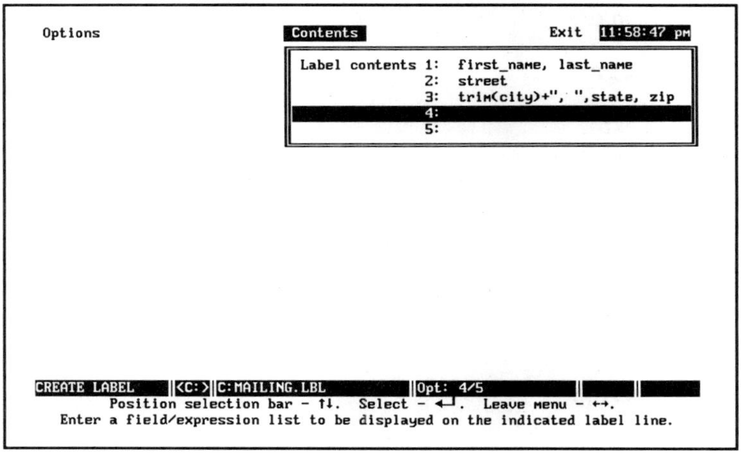

■ *Figure 11.2: Filling in the label contents*

Two or more fields on one line

As you can see, mailing labels often have two or more fields (such as first and last name) on a given line. Since we want the FIRST_NAME and LAST_NAME fields to be printed together on the first line of each label, both of those fields go on line 1 of the form. The comma you see in Figure 11.2 will not appear on the labels, but it is necessary for separating the two field names.

We want the street address to appear on the next line. Simply type in **STREET**—the name of the field that the PHONE database uses for the entire street address—to accomplish this.

Line 3 is the tricky one, because we want to *concatenate* (string together) three fields—CITY, STATE, and ZIP—in such a way that the spacing between them is correct. Since we want the state to appear just a few spaces after the city, we need to cut out any extra spaces in the CITY field before printing the label. Otherwise the city and state line might look like

```
Paris                    ,TX 55493
```

instead of

```
Paris, TX 55493
```

The section of line 3 that reads

```
Trim(CITY)+","
```

strips off extra spaces in the CITY field. Using the plus (+) sign adds a comma and one space to separate the city and the state. The last part of the line tacks the zip code on the end.

Why use commas?

All the "elements" (field names and quote marks) are separated by commas. If you leave out a comma or put one in the wrong place, dBASE will give you this error message when you try to print the labels:

```
Syntax error in contents expression
```

PRINTING THE LABELS

To save your work and print the labels, follow these steps:

1. Press the Enter key until the arrow disappears.
2. Select Exit/Save.
3. Select Retrieve/Label.
4. Choose the drive and the label file name.
5. Note that you can create a search condition or specify a scope at this stage if you choose. You might do this to print labels for, say, only people within a certain zip code range. Select Execute the Command.

You can print selected labels

6. Prepare your printer. It's best to do a trial run on regular paper to make sure that everything is aligned. If your printer has a tractor feeder, you may have to experiment a little to find the right starting position. Then compare the printout to your label paper. Remember, if things are misaligned, you can always press the Esc key to stop the printing.
7. Answer **Y** when the printer asks if you intend to print. The labels will begin rolling out (see Figure 11.3).

```
Randolf Robbins
374 Tipplemeyer Ave.
Cornmont, CA 94709

Adriator Wegwo
158 Snorewell Blvd.
Sleepyhollow, CA 02587

Randy Batterydown
495 Anode St.
Carbondale, IL 30129

Marcel Phillip
456 Fresno St.
Paris, TX 55493

MARIAN DAVIES
344 MARKET ST
NEW YORK, NY 10021

Hank Davies
333 33rd St.
West Goshen, SD 43312

Aretha Phillipson
999 Motor City Ave.
Detroit, MI 39482

Nimrod Neverburger
77 Easy Street
Khozad, CA 89751

Valerie Kuletski
451 Farenheit Ct.
Oakland, CA 95420
```

▪ ***Figure 11.3: Labels from the PHONE database***

MODIFYING A LABEL FORMAT

Just as with database structures and report formats, you can easily modify a label file. It's likely you'll need to—successful label printing usually takes several tries. Just keep modifying and trying again.

1. Select Modify/Label.
2. Specify the drive and file name.
3. Make the changes.
4. Save the file.
5. Try printing your labels again.

If you're having trouble getting the printing lined up correctly on the labels, check the switches on your printer. They are often the culprits, especially if you are getting blank lines between every printed line or if the labels are coming out too wide. In the first instance, it may be that the printer's *local line feed* switch is set to ON. Try turning it off. If you are having the latter problem, your printer may be set for too few characters per inch (e.g., 10 instead of 12), forcing the printing to be too wide. Reset to 12 and try again.

30

Working with Numbers

Previous Steps have shown you the basics of database design, data input, editing, and extraction, as well as how to create reports. The bulk of the examples have focused on text fields. In this Step, we'll cover some more techniques for managing Numeric fields to your best advantage.

You can ask dBASE III PLUS some pretty sophisticated questions about the information in your database. Some of this capability was made evident in Step 7. However, there are other techniques you might want to know about if you intend to work with numbers regularly.

Let's consider the CAMPING database again (see Figure 12.1).

Suppose you want the following information from this database, but you don't want to run a report:

- What is the total cost of all the items?
- What is the total weight of all the items?
- Which of the items cost more than $10.00?
- Which items weigh less than 20 pounds, cost more than $12.50, and are owned by Renee?

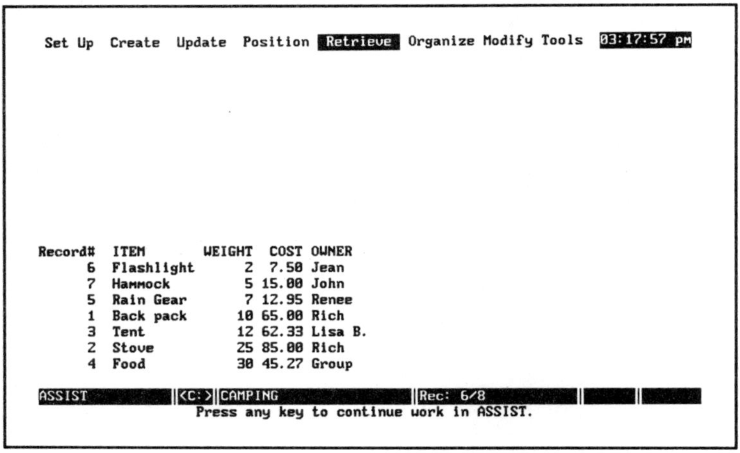

▪ ***Figure 12.1: The CAMPING database***

Operators and functions

The program can answer these and other types of mathematical and logical questions using its built-in *operators* and *functions*. In this Step, we'll discuss the Arithmetic operators, Comparison operators, and arithmetic functions.

USING OPERATORS

You already know something about the Comparison operators from Steps 6 and 7. You might recall that you used some of them when building search conditions for listings. The dBASE program also has built-in Arithmetic operators for performing calculations.

Arithmetic Operators

Let's look at the Arithmetic operators first. The Arithmetic operators in dBASE really amount to a fancy four-function calculator with lots of memory for storing input and answers. You can use the Arithmetic operators to add, subtract, multiply, or divide, just as if you were using a calculator. You can also ask dBASE questions about your databases using these operators.

In the following exercises, the / means "divided by" and the * means "multiplied by." The question marks in the following commands mean "What is the value?"

1. Press Esc enough times to get out of the Assistant and to the dot prompt.
2. Type in the following line:

   ```
   ?3+5
   ```

   and press Enter. The answer, 8, appears on the next line. Continue by entering these equations:

   ```
   ?5/2.5
   ?(3+2)+(14-10)
   ?(3+2)+(14-10)-((12.56+3.5)*(126.23/25))
   ```

   The answer for each will immediately follow:

   ```
   2.00
   9
   -72.0902
   ```

If you analyze the last calculation, you'll notice that the operations enclosed in parentheses are calculated first. Use parentheses carefully to tell dBASE exactly how you want the values calculated. This will ensure proper results.

Now let's try some calculations based on data in the CAMPING database. Suppose you want to know how much the group paid per pound for food. You just apply the appropriate Arithmetic operators to the fields in question. Figure 12.2 shows the commands I used to list the data, move to record 4 (the food record), and then do the calculation.

Notice that the calculation applies only to record 4, the current record. Repositioning the pointer would have given us different results.

Obviously, this was a relatively simple calculation. However, this type of operation can be a real time-saver when you're working with

```
. use camping
. list
Record#  ITEM        WEIGHT  COST OWNER
      1  Back pack       10 65.00 Rich
      2  Stove           25 85.00 Rich
      3  Tent            12 62.33 Lisa B.
      4  Food            30 45.27 Group
      5  Rain Gear        7 12.95 Renee
      6  Flashlight       2  7.50 Jean
      7  Hammock          5 15.00 John

. goto 4
. display
Record#  ITEM        WEIGHT  COST OWNER
      4  Food            30 45.27 Group

. ?cost/weight
    1.51
.
```

▪ ***Figure 12.2: Manually calculating field data***

a larger or more complex database. This is illustrated in the STEREO database examples later in this Step.

Comparison Operators

As mentioned in Step 7, Comparison operators compare two pieces of data to produce a result. You used the Equal To operator to compare character strings earlier. Now we'll look at how Comparison operators can be used to compare numbers. Here are the Comparison operators and their symbols:

Symbol	***Meaning***
=	Equal To
<=	Less Than or Equal To
<	Less Than
>	Greater Than
>=	Greater Than or Equal To
<>	Not Equal To

Suppose you want to list only items that have a wholesale price of $250 or more from the STEREO database. This requires using the Greater Than or Equal To operator. Follow these steps:

1. First open the STEREO database.
2. Select Retrieve/List/Build a Search Condition.
3. Select WHOLESALE from the Fields list.
4. Select >= Greater Than or Equal To.
5. Type in **250.00.**
8. Select No More Conditions.
9. Execute the command. The screen will look like Figure 12.3.

There may be times when you want to eliminate records that don't fall into an acceptable range from a listing, report, or mailing. You can use the <> Not Equal operator to accomplish this. Say you want to do a mailing to everyone in the PHONE database *except* those people living in zip code area 94709, since you've already mailed to that area.

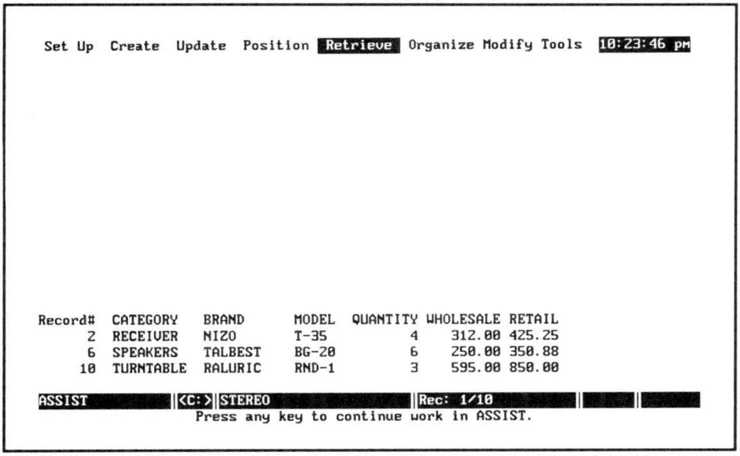

▪ ***Figure 12.3: Using the >= operator to list items of $250 or more***

1. Open the PHONE database.
2. Select Retrieve/List.
3. Construct a Field list of FIRST_NAME, LAST_NAME, and ZIP.
4. Build a search condition, choosing ZIP as the field and <> Not Equal as the operator. Type in **94709.**
5. Select No More Conditions and execute the command.

The result is shown in Figure 12.4. Notice that record 1 is missing —its zip code was 94709.

These examples give you an idea of how to employ the Comparison operators. Keep in mind that you can use them when running not only lists, but labels and reports as well.

THE SUM COMMAND

One of the more useful numeric commands is Sum. Sum calculates a total for *all* the data in the Numeric fields in your database. Most operators work only on the current record.

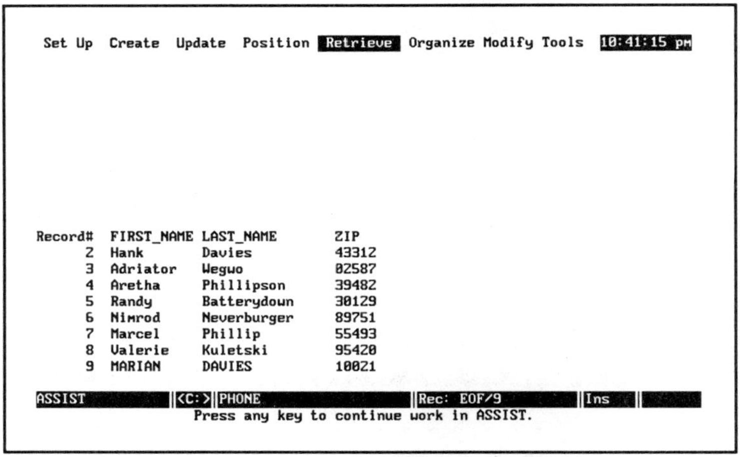

▪ ***Figure 12.4: Eliminating the record with a 94709 zip code***

Suppose you want to quickly see the total quantity, wholesale amount, and retail amount for the stereo store inventory.

1. From the Assistant, select Retrieve/Sum.
2. Execute the command.

The sums are quickly calculated and displayed.

```
10 records summed
QUANTITY    WHOLESALE    RETAIL
     131      1989.40   2919.35
```

Don't forget, you can construct a Field list and/or build a search condition for use with the Sum command, also. You might do this, for example, if you wanted to list sums for turntables only.

CALCULATING AVERAGES

Just below the Sum option in the Retrieve menu is Average. This calculates the arithmetic mean of Numeric fields in the active database. To calculate the mean for the Numeric fields in the STEREO database, follow these steps:

1. Select Retrieve/Average.
2. Execute the command.

The following results are displayed:

```
10 records averaged
QUANTITY  WHOLESALE  RETAIL
      13     198.94  291.94
```

As you can see, averages were calculated for all Numeric fields.

Suppose you are considering carrying a new line of receivers, but the sales rep is quoting a price that seems too high. You can quickly check your average price for receivers by entering this command at the dot prompt:

```
AVERAGE WHOLESALE FOR CATEGORY = "RECEIVER"
```

The program responds:

```
4 records averaged
WHOLESALE
   142.61
```

You can achieve the same results from the Assistant by selecting Retrieve/Average, constructing a Field list, building a search condition with Category = RECEIVER, and executing the command.

MAKING DBASE COUNT

Sometimes you may just want to know how many records meet certain criteria. For example, if you're doing a mailing, you may want to know how many labels will be printed for a specific range of zip codes in order to calculate the number of labels to buy and the postage required. The combinations are limitless, but when you need to know "How many?" you can use the Count command.

Simply choosing Retrieve/Count/Execute the Command for the PHONE database has the following effect:

```
10 records
```

Since we didn't specify any criteria, dBASE counted only the number of records in the database.

Conditional counting

Setting up a more complex count requires building a condition. To count the number of labels needed for a range of zip codes, you could, for example, type at the dot prompt

```
COUNT FOR ZIP >= 90000 .AND. ZIP <= 99999
```

and press Enter. This type of count can also be achieved from the Assistant by building a search condition before executing the Count command.

The program will issue an error message

```
Data type mismatch
```

if you try to use this command on a zip code field like the one in the PHONE database. This is because the <= and >= operators are attempting to do a numeric comparison on a Character field. If your zip code field is a Character field rather than Numeric field, replace the word *ZIP* (or whatever name you've assigned to your zip code field) with *VAL(ZIP)*. This temporarily converts the Character field data to numeric values in order to perform the comparisons. Thus the command would be

Converting characters to numbers

```
COUNT FOR VAL(ZIP)>=90000 .AND. VAL(ZIP) <= 99999
```

30

Working with Dates

Step 12 explained some of the more salient points to remember when using Numeric fields. This Step will discuss another type of number—dates. You'll learn how to add a Date field to your database structure, how to enter dates, and how to use dBASE to do calculations and reporting based on dates.

Next to the values in Numeric fields, dates may be the most important form of data in many business databases. Whether you're keeping track of sales, payables and receivables, clients, or project scheduling, you'll often want to store and retrieve information covering a certain period of time. The dBASE program provides the tools for keeping track of dates and for doing the necessary date calculations.

DATE FIELD BASICS

Date fields are always eight spaces long. This leaves room for the slash mark (/) between each of the three components (e.g., 12/14/92). Dates may range from 01/01/01 A.D. upward.

Date formats

As shipped in the U.S., dBASE is set to use dates in the mm/dd/yy format. This can be changed, however, from the dot prompt. To choose another format, type

```
SET DATE
```

and a country name selected from the list below. Press Enter. The right column shows the corresponding date format.

AMERICAN	mm/dd/yy
ANSI	yy.mm.dd
BRITISH	dd/mm/yy
FRENCH	dd/mm/yy
GERMAN	dd.mm.yy
ITALIAN	dd-mm-yy

Slashes entered automatically

When you enter data in a Date field, dBASE puts in the / marks for you. You just type in the numbers and the cursor skips right over the / marks to make data entry convenient. If you try to enter an erroneous date, such as 2/29/90, dBASE will reject it and ask for a new entry (February of 1990 didn't have 29 days).

The program will leave the first two digits of the century off unless you specify otherwise. You might want to change that if you expect to be using dates of other centuries. To display all four digits, from the dot prompt type

```
SET CENTURY ON
```

and press Enter. To reverse the effect, type

```
SET CENTURY OFF
```

USING A DATE FIELD FOR CONDITIONAL SEARCHING

Suppose we wanted to see items in the STEREO database that were ordered between 1990 and 1992 (that is, were ordered in 1991). To prepare for this conditional search, I've added a Date field called LAST_ORDER to the STEREO database to show when each product was last ordered. I've also entered the dates. Now the listed data looks like Figure 13.1.

1. Select Retrieve/List/Build a Search Condition.
2. Select LAST_ORDER.
3. Select < Less Than.
4. Type in **01/01/92**. (You have to type in the / marks here.)
5. Select Combine with .AND.
6. Select LAST_ORDER from the Fields list again.
7. Select > Greater Than.
8. Type in **12/31/90**.
9. Select No More Conditions.
10. Execute the command. You will see the following results:

    SPEAKERS RAZCO L-55 30 199.99 249.00 03/01/85

In effect, we told dBASE: "Show all the records where the dates fall between December 31, 1990 and January 1, 1992." This technique

```
Set Up  Create  Update  Position  Retrieve  Organize  Modify  Tools  02:55:34 am

Record#  CATEGORY    BRAND      MODEL   QUANTITY WHOLESALE RETAIL LAST_ORDER
      1  RECEIVER    NIZO       T-33           5    225.49 350.49 01/12/92
      2  RECEIVER    NIZO       T-35           4    312.00 425.25 01/12/92
      3  RECEIVER    ACME       RZ5-MT        13     19.99  49.99 05/15/92
      4  RECEIVER    NADIR      2-CHP         50     12.95  29.99 03/06/53
      5  SPEAKERS    RAZCO      L-55          30    199.00 249.00 03/01/91
      6  SPEAKERS    TALBEST    BG-20          6    250.00 350.88 07/13/92
      7  TAPE DECK   ROLLEM     CAS-3         10    125.65 212.99 09/01/92
      8  TAPE DECK   FLOWUTTER  WBL-5          5    149.33 250.77 09/15/92
      9  TURNTABLE   XIRTAM     25-L           5     99.99 149.99 02/28/90
     10  TURNTABLE   RALURIC    RND-1          3    595.00 850.00 10/01/92

ASSIST            ||<C:>||STEREO              ||Rec: 1/10     ||     ||
                  Press any key to continue work in ASSIST.
```

■ ***Figure 13.1: The STEREO database with dates added***

can be used to select records for quarterly sales figures, tax preparation, or what have you. Basing your search condition on Date fields allows you to print reports showing what happened when.

USING DATE FUNCTIONS FROM THE DOT PROMPT

There are a few functions built into dBASE for manipulating dates. You can use these in conjunction with Date fields to create more complex search conditions.

Table 13.1 lists the date functions and examples of their results.

Function	*Effect*
DOW	The day of the week in numbers (Sunday = 1)
CDOW	The day of the week in characters (Friday)
DAY	The day of the month (03)
MONTH	The month in numbers (1-12)
CMONTH	The month in characters (March)
YEAR	The year (1992)
DATE()	The current system date

Table 13.1: Date functions

These functions can be used only from the dot prompt. Here are some examples to illustrate their usefulness.

Using DOW

Suppose you wanted to see all the orders that were placed on a Friday. You could apply the DOW (day of the week) function to the LAST_ORDER field and specify 6 as the day.

```
LIST FOR DOW(LAST_ORDER) = 6
```

The result is shown in Figure 13.2

```
. list for dow(last_order)=6
Record#  CATEGORY   BRAND      MODEL   QUANTITY WHOLESALE RETAIL LAST_ORDER
      3  RECEIVER   ACME       R25-MT        13     19.99  49.99 05/15/92
      4  RECEIVER   NADIR      Z-CHP         50     12.95  29.99 03/06/53
      5  SPEAKERS   RAZCO      L-55          30    199.00 249.00 03/01/91

.
Command Line    ||<C:>||STEREO               ||Rec: EOF/10       ||      ||
                      Enter a dBASE III PLUS command.
```

▪ *Figure 13.2: Orders placed on Fridays*

You could translate the search condition this way: "List a record if the day-of-the-week value of the last-order date is equal to six (Friday)."

Using CDOW

Now let's try the same thing using the CDOW function. Just substitute the name of the day:

```
LIST FOR CDOW(LAST_ORDER) = "FRIDAY"
```

The response is the same as in Figure 13.2.

Using DAY

To show all orders placed on the 15th of the month, type

```
LIST FOR DAY(LAST_ORDER) = 15
```

Using MONTH and CMONTH

To see all orders placed in March of any year, type

```
LIST FOR MONTH(LAST_ORDER) = 3
```

or

```
LIST FOR CMONTH(LAST_ORDER) = "MARCH"
```

Recall that in an example in Step 7 search criteria specifying beginning and ending dates were combined with the .AND. operator. The YEAR function provides an easier way to see items which were last ordered in 1991:

Using YEAR

```
LIST FOR YEAR(LAST_ORDER) = 1991
```

Using DATE( )

Finally, there is DATE(), the system date function. When you use this function, it is much like typing *date* at the dot prompt. The difference is that you can use DATE() from within dBASE. From the dot prompt, type

```
? DATE()
```

and press Enter. You'll get something like this:

```
06/06/92
```

The date displayed on *your* screen, of course, will be the current date. You can use the system date as a comparison for dates stored in your database. Typically this is done to list events which occurred "today," such as listing today's sales from a transaction account. If we want to see all the orders placed today, the command would look like this:

```
LIST FOR LAST_ORDER = DATE()
```

If you want to print out the results of *any* listing you make from the dot prompt, regardless of whether dates are involved, add the words *to print* at the end of the command. For example:

```
LIST FOR DAY(LAST_ORDER) = 15 TO PRINT
```

DATE CALCULATIONS

Using the Arithmetic operators, you can do date calculations. Suppose you wanted to know how many days have passed since you last ordered an item. You could sit down with a calendar and count the days, or you could ask dBASE to calculate it for you. Here's an example using the STEREO database.

```
LIST DATE()-LAST_ORDER FOR CATEGORY ="RECEIVER"
```

Assuming today is 06/06/92, dBASE responds

Record #	DATE()-LAST_ORDER
1	146
2	146
3	22
4	14337

Let's say you decide to put your ordering on a 30-day schedule. How could you easily tell which items were overdue for a reorder?

```
LIST FOR DATE()-LAST_ORDER >= 30
```

The command translates: "Show records for which today minus the last-order date is equal to or greater than 30 days." The results are shown in Figure 13.3.

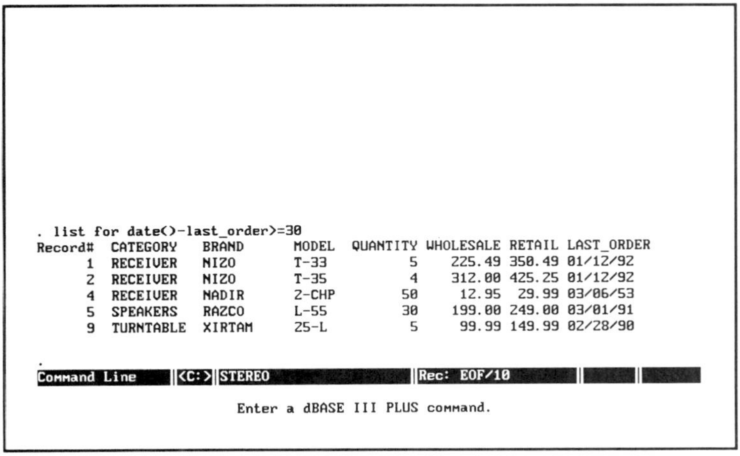

```
. list for date()-last_order>=30
Record#  CATEGORY   BRAND      MODEL  QUANTITY WHOLESALE RETAIL LAST_ORDER
      1  RECEIVER   NIZO       T-33          5    225.49 350.49 01/12/92
      2  RECEIVER   NIZO       T-35          4    312.00 425.25 01/12/92
      4  RECEIVER   NADIR      Z-CHP        50     12.95  29.99 03/06/53
      5  SPEAKERS   RAZCO      L-55         30    199.00 249.00 03/01/91
      9  TURNTABLE  XIRTAM     25-L          5     99.99 149.99 02/28/90

.
Command Line  <C:> STEREO            Rec: EOF/10

                    Enter a dBASE III PLUS command.
```

■ ***Figure 13.3: Listing items not ordered for 30 days or more***

Using CTOD

You can also calculate the number of elapsed days between two dates. To do this, use the CTOD function. For example, to see how many days have passed between the signing of the Declaration of Independence and the celebration of the restoration of the Statue of Liberty, type

```
? CTOD("07/04/1986")-CTOD("07/04/1776")
```

The program calculates and displays the answer:

```
76700
```

SORTING AND INDEXING ON DATE FIELDS

It's frequently necessary to order your files by date. You can sort or index by dates to achieve this effect. Sorting can be done in either ascending or descending order; however, you can index only in ascending order.

Figure 13.4 shows the result of indexing on the Date field. Notice that the indexing was done from the dot prompt rather than from the Assistant.

```
. index on last_order to dateup
  100% indexed          10 Records indexed
. list
Record#  CATEGORY   BRAND      MODEL   QUANTITY WHOLESALE RETAIL LAST_ORDER
      4  RECEIVER   NADIR      Z-CHP         50     12.95  29.99 03/06/53
      9  TURNTABLE  XIRTAM     Z5-L           5     99.99 149.99 02/28/90
      5  SPEAKERS   RAZCO      L-55          30    199.00 249.00 03/01/91
      1  RECEIVER   NIZO       T-33           5    225.49 350.49 01/12/92
      2  RECEIVER   NIZO       T-35           4    312.00 425.25 01/12/92
      3  RECEIVER   ACME       R25-MT        13     19.99  49.99 05/15/92
      6  SPEAKERS   TALBEST    BG-20          6    250.00 350.88 07/13/92
      7  TAPE DECK  ROLLEM     CAS-3         10    125.65 212.99 09/01/92
      8  TAPE DECK  FLOWUTTER  WBL-5          5    149.33 250.77 09/15/92
     10  TURNTABLE  RALURIC    RND-1          3    595.00 850.00 10/01/92

.
Command Line    <C:> STEREO                Rec: EOF/10

                 Enter a dBASE III PLUS command.
```

■ *Figure 13.4: Records in order of ascending dates*

30

Working with Logical Fields

In the last Step you learned how dBASE can use dates. This Step introduces a new data type—Logical fields. Logical fields are useful for keeping track of things like "Did Ted's parents like this recipe enough to have it again?", "Did this check bounce?", or "Is this donation tax-deductible?" You could achieve the same results using Character fields, but it's easier to use Logical fields. They are also faster, because dBASE has Logical field functions that will speed up your work.

ADDING LOGICAL FIELDS TO YOUR DATABASE

By definition, Logical fields can answer only one kind of question: "Is this true or false?" Thus, Logical fields are only one character wide—just large enough to contain a *T* or an *F* (for true or false) or, alternatively, a *Y* or an *N* (for yes or no).

To illustrate the concept and utility of Logical fields, I've added one to the STEREO database. (To refresh your memory about adding fields, refer to Step 4.) Let's assume there are certain items that you sell only via interstate marketing and shipping. Therefore, you don't collect state sales tax on these items. In this situation, a Logical field could indicate whether or not sales tax should be added when figuring the total sales price of each product. I've also added a field to hold the total price, which would include the sales tax, if applicable. There are now nine fields in the STEREO database, as shown in Figure 14.1.

Now we can have dBASE compute the total price of the item based on whether tax should be added or not, as indicated by the contents of each record's Logical field.

Default value of Logical fields

When you add a Logical field to a structure, dBASE automatically enters "F" (False) in the field for all existing records. You must edit the records if you want them to hold T. If you choose, you can use Y instead of T, and N instead of F.

Note in Figure 14.2 that I've added some information in the new Logical field, TAX, for each record

```
                                                 Bytes remaining:   3941

   Field Name  Type       Width  Dec          Field Name  Type      Width  Dec
   ==================================          ==================================
 1 CATEGORY    Character   10
 2 BRAND       Character   10
 3 MODEL       Character    6
 4 QUANTITY    Numeric      6     0
 5 WHOLESALE   Numeric      6     2
 6 RETAIL      Numeric      6     2
 7 LAST_ORDER  Date         8
 8 TAX         Logical      1
 9 TOTAL       Numeric      6     2

MODIFY STRUCTURE |<C:>|STEREO              |Field: 9/9       |      |Num
                         Enter the field name.
Field names begin with a letter and may contain letters, digits and underscores
```

- ***Figure 14.1: The STEREO database structure with two new fields (no indexes on)***

```
CATEGORY-- BRAND----- MODEL- QUANTITY WHOLESALE RETAIL LAST_ORDER TAX TOTAL-
RECEIVER   NIZO       T-33          5    225.49 350.49 01/12/92   T      0.00
RECEIVER   NIZO       T-35          4    312.00 425.25 01/12/92   T      0.00
RECEIVER   ACME       R25-MT       13     19.99  49.99 05/15/92   F      0.00
RECEIVER   NADIR      Z-CHP        50     12.95  29.99 03/06/53   T      0.00
SPEAKERS   RAZCO      L-55         30    199.00 249.00 03/01/91   F      0.00
SPEAKERS   TALBEST    BG-20         6    250.00 350.88 07/13/92   T      0.00
TAPE DECK  ROLLEM     CAS-3        10    125.65 212.99 09/01/92   T      0.00
TAPE DECK  FLOWUTTER  WBL-5         5    149.33 250.77 09/15/92   F      0.00
TURNTABLE  XIRTAM     Z5-L          5     99.99 149.99 02/28/90   T      0.00
TURNTABLE  RALURIC    RND-1         3    595.00 850.00 10/01/92   F      0.00

BROWSE         <C:> STEREO                 Rec: 10/10              Num
                         ===> Add new records? (Y/N)
                            View and edit fields.
```

■ *Figure 14.2: The TAX field, filled in*

Now that we have nine fields, the listings wrap on the screen. To temporarily eliminate some fields from the listings, try a new command called Set Fields. Type

Using Set Fields

SET FIELDS TO CATEGORY, BRAND, MODEL, RETAIL, TAX, TOTAL

This causes only the specified fields to show when you use the List, Display, and Browse options.

Don't forget to turn off the Set Fields command before running a report; otherwise, some fields won't show up. Type

SET FIELDS OFF

FINDING DATA WITH LOGICAL FIELDS

Now say you want to see which items need tax added to them, and which don't. It's fastest to work from the dot prompt, though you can achieve the same results from the Assistant. To show the items that are taxable, from the dot prompt type

Listing true or false records

```
LIST FOR TAX
```

and press Enter.

To show nontaxable items, type

```
LIST FOR .NOT. TAX
```

and press Enter.

The results of both operations are listed in Figure 14.3.

The .NOT. operator

To list the records in the nontaxable category we used a new operator, called the NOT operator. It's a Logical operator that *excludes,* rather than includes, a condition. In effect, it does what the word *not* does in normal English and reverses part of the command. You might think of the second command above as "List records where TAX does *not* equal T." Since "not true" is the same as "false," this amounts to "List the records where TAX equals F."

```
. list for tax
Record#  CATEGORY   BRAND      MODEL   RETAIL TAX  TOTAL
      1  RECEIVER   NIZO       T-33    350.49 .T.
      2  RECEIVER   NIZO       T-35    425.25 .T.
      4  RECEIVER   NADIR      Z-CHP    29.99 .T.
      6  SPEAKERS   TALBEST    BG-20   350.88 .T.
      7  TAPE DECK  ROLLEM     CAS-3   212.99 .T.
      9  TURNTABLE  XIRTAM     25-L    149.99 .T.

. list for .not. tax
Record#  CATEGORY   BRAND      MODEL   RETAIL TAX  TOTAL
      3  RECEIVER   ACME       R25-MT   49.99 .F.
      5  SPEAKERS   RAZCO      L-55    249.00 .F.
      8  TAPE DECK  FLOWUTTER  WBL-5   250.77 .F.
     10  TURNTABLE  RALURIC     RND-1  850.00 .F.

.
Command Line   <C:> STEREO              Rec: EOF/10              Num
                   Enter a dBASE III PLUS command.
```

■ *Figure 14.3: Records in both taxable and nontaxable categories*

MAKING FILE-WIDE CHANGES

You can also use Logical fields as "switches" to control other operations. For example, now that all of the records in the database have a T or an F setting for TAX, we can have dBASE calculate the total sales amount for each item. We can instruct dBASE to look at the TAX field and add tax if appropriate, or leave it out, based on the settings.

Adding sales tax

Here's how it works. We create a command that says: "Look at each record. If TAX is true, multiply the value in RETAIL by 7% (assuming that's the state sales tax) and store that product in the TOTAL column." You can tell dBASE to store information that it produces in this fashion in a field by using another command, called Replace. For this example, type

```
REPLACE ALL TOTAL WITH RETAIL *.07 FOR TAX
```

and press Enter. The program responds

```
6 records replaced
```

A listing of the results is shown in Figure 14.4

```
. replace all total with retail *.07 for tax
      6 records replaced
. list
Record#  CATEGORY    BRAND       MODEL   RETAIL TAX   TOTAL
      1  RECEIVER    NIZO        T-33    350.49 .T.   24.53
      2  RECEIVER    NIZO        T-35    425.25 .T.   29.77
      3  RECEIVER    ACME        R25-MT   49.99 .F.
      4  RECEIVER    NADIR       Z-CHP    29.99 .T.    2.10
      5  SPEAKERS    RAZCO       L-55    249.00 .F.
      6  SPEAKERS    TALBEST     BG-20   350.88 .T.   24.56
      7  TAPE DECK   ROLLEM      CAS-3   212.99 .T.   14.91
      8  TAPE DECK   FLOWUTTER   WBL-5   250.77 .F.
      9  TURNTABLE   XIRTAM      25-L    149.99 .T.   10.50
     10  TURNTABLE   RALURIC      RND-1  850.00 .F.

.
Command Line  |<C:>|STEREO          |Rec: EOF/10     |     |Num

                    Enter a dBASE III PLUS command.
```

■ ***Figure 14.4: The results of the replacements based on TAX***

STEP 14

Oops! That was wrong, wasn't it? Notice that TOTAL only shows the tax, not the total amount. The formula has to be changed to

```
REPLACE ALL TOTAL WITH RETAIL + (RETAIL *.07)
FOR TAX
```

or

```
REPLACE ALL TOTAL WITH (RETAIL *1.07) FOR TAX
```

Either one will work. Finally, I went ahead and put prices in for the nontaxable items using a modification of the formula.

```
REPLACE ALL TOTAL WITH RETAIL FOR .NOT. TAX
```

This replaces the current contents of the TOTAL field with the contents of the RETAIL field for each record that is nontaxable. The results of these two operations are shown in Figure 14.5.

These results could have been achieved from the Assistant; however, you'd have to take several more steps to accomplish these tasks. Were you to use the Assistant for this last operation, you would use the

```
. replace all total with retail *1.07 for tax
      6 records replaced
. replace all total with retail for .not. tax
      4 records replaced
. list
Record#  CATEGORY    BRAND      MODEL   RETAIL TAX  TOTAL
      1  RECEIVER    NIZO       T-33    350.49 .T. 375.02
      2  RECEIVER    NIZO       T-35    425.25 .T. 455.02
      3  RECEIVER    ACME       RZ5-MT   49.99 .F.  49.99
      4  RECEIVER    NADIR      Z-CHP    29.99 .T.  32.09
      5  SPEAKERS    RAZCO      L-55    249.00 .F. 249.00
      6  SPEAKERS    TALBEST    BG-20   350.88 .T. 375.44
      7  TAPE DECK   ROLLEM     CAS-3   212.99 .T. 227.90
      8  TAPE DECK   FLOWUTTER  WBL-5   250.77 .F. 250.77
      9  TURNTABLE   XIRTAM     Z5-L    149.99 .T. 160.49
     10  TURNTABLE   RALURIC     RND-1 850.00 .F. 850.00
.
Command Line  |<C:>|STEREO          |Rec: EOF/10     |Ins  |Num
                 Enter a dBASE III PLUS command.
```

■ *Figure 14.5: The records updated with the correct formula*

Replace command on the Update menu. Then you'd follow the prompts at the bottom of the screen to determine what steps to take.

Additional uses for Logical fields

As with all the other fields types and functions, you can use Logical fields as search criteria for reports, mailing labels, and other operations such as deleting or recalling records. Logical fields may also be used in conjunction with other search criteria via the .AND. and .OR. operators.

Using Memo Fields

This Step shows you how to create a Memo field, how to add textual information to it, and how to edit that text.

WHEN TO USE A MEMO FIELD

When discussing the size of fields in a database, I said that you should be careful not to make fields any longer than necessary, in order to avoid wasting disk space. But what if you sometimes need to store extended information for just a few records? You could add one long character field (up to 254 characters wide) to your database structure. However, you'd be using up 254 bytes of space for *each and every* record, regardless of whether you use the field of not. That's a lot of wasted space on your data disk, and it increases very quickly as you add records.

The better solution is a Memo field. Memo fields actually contain pointers only, so they are quite small. The pointers refer to a secondary disk file that holds the memos. This file is much more space-efficient than a Character field, growing only as you add information. If you have just a few memos in your database, then the associated memo file remains small. The result is that very little space is taken up on your disk, and none of it is wasted.

Memo field files are given the same first name as their main database, but an extension *.DBT* (database text) is added.

ADDING A MEMO FIELD

Say you've just received a letter from the famous writer, Randolf Robbins, announcing that he will be working under a new pen name, Wackford Squeers. You'll want to change his name in your PHONE database and make some annotation about the reason for the change. You can do this by adding a Memo field, but first you need to prepare the database.

1. Open the PHONE database.
2. When asked about the index, answer **N**.
3. Select Organize/Index.
4. Type **FIRST_NAME** to create a first name index.
5. Select the appropriate drive and name the index file **FIRST**.
6. Create another index called **LAST,** based on LAST_NAME.
7. Create a third index called **COMP,** based on COMPANY.
8. Now open the database again. From the Setup/Database File command, choose PHONE and the indexes FIRST, LAST, and COMP, in that order. Notice how the Assistant adds *Master* to the name of the first chosen index, FIRST, and appends *02* and *03* to the other two. This indicates that the FIRST index controls the order of records.

Now we'll add the Memo field.

1. Choose Modify/Database File, or from the dot prompt type

   ```
   MODIFY STRUCTURE
   ```

2. Alter the structure to look like Figure 15.1 by adding a Memo field called NOTES. (The default width is 10. You can't change this, but remember that the Memo field holds only the pointers.)

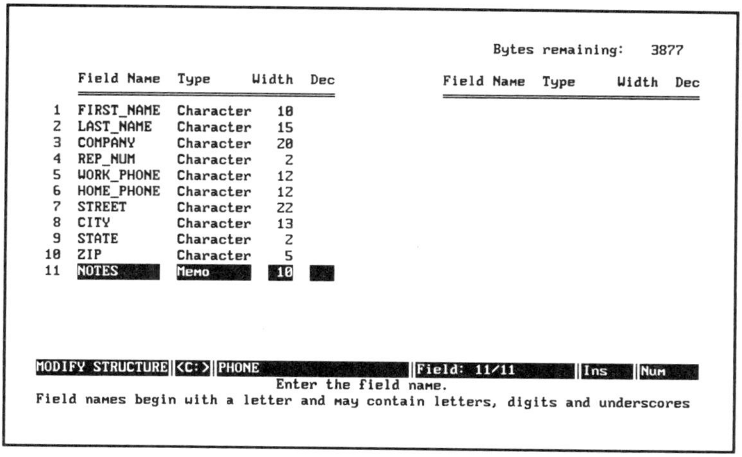

▪ ***Figure 15.1: Adding a Memo field to the PHONE database***

3. Save the modified structure.
4. Return to the Assistant. Choose Position/Seek and enter **Randolf** to get to Randolf Robbins's record.
5. Choose Update/Edit to see the record.
6. Alter the FIRST_NAME and LAST_NAME fields to read **Wackford Squeers**.
7. Move down to the newly added Memo field with ↓.
8. Once the cursor is on the Memo field, press Ctrl-Home. The screen changes to the *Memo Editor screen.* Press F1 to see the editing keys if they aren't already showing. (Most of the editing keys are the same as those already described for the Edit and Browse modes.)
9. Type in some notes about the name change, as shown in Figure 15.2. Try using the editing codes to move around word by word, line by line, from the end of the line to the beginning of the line, and so forth, as indicated in the Help box at the top of the screen.

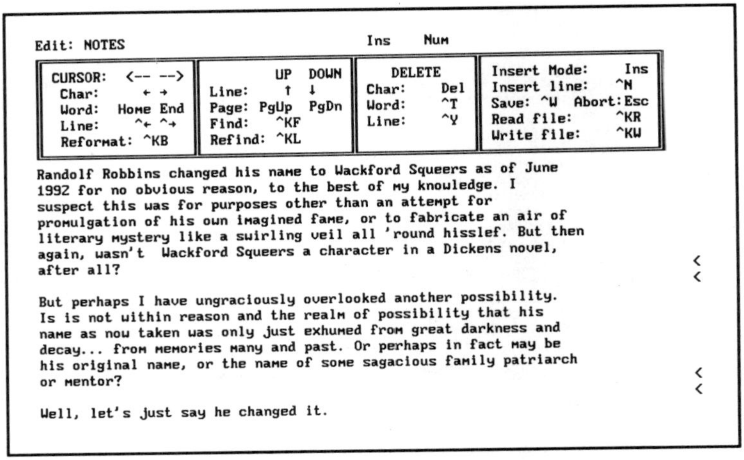

■ *Figure 15.2: Making some notes in a Memo field*

10. Save the memo when you are done. If you do not save it, it will be lost.

ENTERING TEXT IN MEMO FIELDS

There are a few things to remember about memos. As you enter information in them, your words will wrap around automatically from line to line. Press Enter only to begin a new paragraph, not for each line. The Memo Editor will take care of the line breaks for you.

Refor-matting paragraphs

Each paragraph is considered by the Memo Editor to be a separate entity. As you edit them, they may fall out of format: lines of text may push off the right side of the screen or seem too long or too short. Often, a small + sign will appear in the right margin, marking where words break before continuing on the next line. You can reformat the paragraph by placing the cursor in it and pressing Ctrl-K-B; that is, by holding down Ctrl and then pressing K, followed by B.

ASCII FILES AND MEMOS

You can copy an existing text file (note that it must be in ASCII text format) into a Memo file using the Ctrl-K-R command.

Reading ASCII files into memos

1. Position the cursor where you want to place the text file.
2. Issue the command by pressing Ctrl-K-R.
3. The Memo Editor asks you the name of the file. Type it in and press Enter. The file is copied into the memo at the point of the cursor. The original ASCII file is left unaltered.

You can also write a memo to disk as a file. This is useful when you want to pull the information from a dBASE memo into another program, such as a word processor.

1. Type Ctrl-K-W.
2. The Memo Editor asks for a file name. Type in the name and press Enter. The current memo is written into a file of that name on disk (in the currently active DOS directory for that drive, unless you specify an entire path name that includes another directory name).

CARING FOR MEMO FILES

Take care of your Memo files. When you make copies of your database files to be used on another computer or from another disk, be sure to copy your Memo (*.DBT*) files too.

Also, don't alter your database until you've stored the accompanying Memo file in the same directory. Otherwise, the record pointers will not be updated when you add or delete records in the main database and the link between the two files will be corrupted. Once the record pointers are mixed up, memos end up being associated with the wrong records, which gets pretty confusing. Sometimes the Memo file won't work at all. And unlike indexes, which can be rebuilt by simply reindexing, Memo files can't be easily or quickly fixed.

60

Working with Multiple Databases—Appending

So far, all the commands and techniques we've covered have involved single databases. Most people use only one database at a time, just as they use only a single word-processing document at a time. However, there are situations that call for the use of several databases together. This Step covers one technique for using multiple databases—appending. Step 17 covers another approach, linking.

In this Step, we'll discuss

- Merging data from one file into another
- Using two or more databases at the same time

MERGING DATA WITH APPEND

You've already used the Append command to manually add records to a database. However, the Append command can also pull records from an existing database into the current one, eliminating the possibility of duplication.

To illustrate how merging works, let's say that you own the stereo store of our earlier examples. You've just acquired another store, which sells TVs. Your stores are doing well, but space is getting cramped in both small store locations. You decide to merge the two stores together in a new, large storefront operation. It then makes sense to merge the databases as well.

Figure 16.1 shows the TV store's database structure and its contents. (I listed the structure with the Display Structure command.)

Note that our two databases, STEREO and TV, have similar structures, though not identical ones. There are, however, some identical fields, though their orders are reversed. Others are absent from the TV database , and the TV file has a field (SIZE) not included in the STEREO file at all.

To pull records into the STEREO database from the TV database, go to the dot prompt and type

```
APPEND FROM TV
```

The program reports the number of records added, as you see in Figure 16.2. The figure also shows a listing of all the records now in the STEREO database, including the five pulled in from the TV database. Use the List Off command to list the data without the

```
Number of data records:        6
Date of last update   : 06/08/92
Field  Field Name  Type       Width    Dec
    1  CATEGORY    Character     10
    2  BRAND       Character     10
    3  MODEL       Character      6
    4  SIZE        Character      3
    5  QUANTITY    Numeric        2
    6  RETAIL      Numeric        6      2
    7  WHOLESALE   Numeric        6      2
** Total **                      44

. list
Record#  CATEGORY   BRAND      MODEL  SIZE QUANTITY RETAIL WHOLESALE
      1  TELEVISION BLABBEX    KZZ    14"        29 249.99    189.99
      2  TELEVISION BIG-VUE    BV-45  19"         5 750.00    595.00
      3  VCR        CINOSANAP  TP-120             3 345.89    540.99
      4  VIDEO TAPE MAXWELL    XX-120            45   4.99      3.49
      5  VCR        THINEX     TV-29             14 199.00    149.00
      6

.
Command Line  |<C:>|TV                      |Rec: EOF/6        |Ins  |Num

                     Enter a dBASE III PLUS command.
```

■ *Figure 16.1: The TV database*

record numbers so that all the fields can fit on the screen.

The TV database still exists in its original form on the source disk. This is true whenever you append from an outside file.

Source file stays intact

Adding five records was fast. The appending process can take more time, though, if you are appending from a large database. Since you are actually making copies of records, remember that will take a lot of disk space, too.

Improving Your Results

When you append records from another file, there are some things to keep in mind. In our example, there were similar field names and structures. Thus, dBASE knew where to put the data it imported. This wasn't just a happy accident—I intentionally made these elements similar to prepare for a future merge. The results of the merge would have been much less predictable otherwise. As it was, we lost the SIZE field data.

```
. append from TV
      6 records added
. list off
 CATEGORY   BRAND     MODEL   QUANTITY WHOLESALE RETAIL LAST_ORDER TAX  TOTAL
 RECEIVER   NIZO      T-33           5    225.49 350.49 05/15/92   .T. 375.02
 RECEIVER   NIZO      T-35           4    312.00 425.25 01/12/92   .T. 455.02
 RECEIVER   ACME      R25-MT        13     19.99  49.99 01/12/92   .F.  49.99
 RECEIVER   NADIR     Z-CHP         50     12.95  29.99 03/06/53   .T.  32.09
 SPEAKERS   RAZCO     L-55          30    199.00 249.00 07/13/92   .F. 249.00
 SPEAKERS   TALBEST   BG-20          6    250.00 350.88 03/01/91   .T. 375.44
 TAPE DECK  ROLLEM    CAS-3         10    125.65 212.99 09/15/92   .T. 227.90
 TAPE DECK  FLOWUTTER WBL-5          5    149.33 250.77 09/01/92   .F. 250.77
 TURNTABLE  XIRTAM    25-L           5     99.99 149.99 10/01/92   .T. 160.49
 TURNTABLE  RALURIC    RND-1         3    595.00 850.00 02/28/90   .F. 850.00
 TELEVISION BLABBEX   K22           29    189.99 249.99   /  /     .F.
 TELEVISION BIG-VUE   BV-45          5    595.00 750.00   /  /     .F.
 VCR        CINOSANAP TP-120         3    540.99 345.89   /  /     .F.
 VIDEO TAPE MAXWELL   XX-120        45      3.49   4.99   /  /     .F.
 VCR        THINEX    TV-29         14    149.00 199.00   /  /     .F.

.
Command Line  ||<C:>||STEREO          ||Rec: EOF/16       ||Ins  ||Num

                  Enter a dBASE III PLUS command.
```

■ *Figure 16.2: Five records are appended from the TV database*

Use similar field names and structures

Note that dBASE recognized that RETAIL and WHOLESALE were reversed in the TV file and reordered those fields before pulling them into the STEREO file. However, there's not much dBASE can do if no information exists. The TAX field, which does not exist in the TV database, is stuffed with Fs (remember, that's the default setting for Logical fields) and the LAST_ORDER and TOTAL dates were left blank. To prevent losing the data in the SIZE field, you would need to modify the destination database structure (in this case, STEREO) to include a SIZE field before using the Append command.

To understand how dBASE deals with discrepancies while appending, consider how dBASE actually reads in outside records. First, it compares the structure of the two databases concerned. Only fields with the same names are appended; the others are skipped over. If the data to be appended is too long to fit into its new field, it is shortened, or truncated, until it fits. This means you could lose the right-hand portion of some longer entries.

Appending Selected Records

Suppose that instead of appending all the records from the second database you wanted to append only selected ones, such as those for TV sets. Here's a command that would do that:

```
APPEND FROM TV FOR CATEGORY = "TELEVISION"
```

Be sure to specify both the name of the database containing the information you want to append and the record category.

OPENING MULTIPLE DATABASES

When working with database applications, it's not uncommon to need two or more data files open simultaneously. With dBASE, you can have as many as ten *workareas* open simultaneously, each with its own database and indexes active.

To illustrate, here are some examples. Note that in all cases you must work from the dot prompt. Workareas are assigned numbers 1 through 10.

- To open the PHONE database in workarea 1, type

  `USE PHONE`

- Type

  `SELECT 2`

  to switch to workarea 2.

- To open the STEREO database in workarea 2 and activate an index called DATE, type

  `USE STEREO INDEX DATE`

- To show which workarea you are in, press F6 or type

  `DISPLAY STATUS`

- To close all open databases, type

  `CLOSE ALL`

Now move to Step 17 to learn about another method for using multiple databases, linking.

30

Working with Multiple Databases—Linking

Sometimes you may want to work with two or more databases as if they were a single database. If databases have a common field with matching data, DBASE III PLUS lets you link the two databases together to give the impression of having a larger database with more fields in it. While the files are linked, or *related,* you can work with their fields as though they were in the same database. This linking relationship is called a *View.*

ESTABLISHING THE LINK

A common field

When linking two databases, the main thing to remember is that a common field between the two databases is required. Otherwise, the databases will remain unrelated. It is also important that the second database be indexed on the linking field, so that dBASE can quickly find the record that corresponds with the current record in the first database.

Now for an example. Let's say that for each item sold in Uncle Bob's Stereo/TV Store there is a sales representative whom you deal with and order from. When you look at your inventory database to see whether you'll need to order more items, you also want to see the names, addresses, and phone numbers of these folks. However, you don't want to have this information actually stored in the inventory database. Linking the STORE database to a database containing the rep information can solve this problem.

Creating a Common Field

1. To create the link I've described, we'll first have to add a field to the database holding the sales representative information, PHONE. (Now you know who those people are!) This new field will hold the data used to link the two databases. I'll call it REP_NUM and designate it a Character field with a width of 2. Enter the data shown in Figure 17.1.

Indexing the linked file

2. As I mentioned earlier, the second (or linked) file has to be indexed by the linking field. For our example, we have to index PHONE by REP_NUM using the Organize/Index command. I've called the index REPS.
3. The other database (STEREO) needs to have a (REP_NUM) field too, with a rep number assigned to each item. Figure 17.2 shows the necessary modifications.

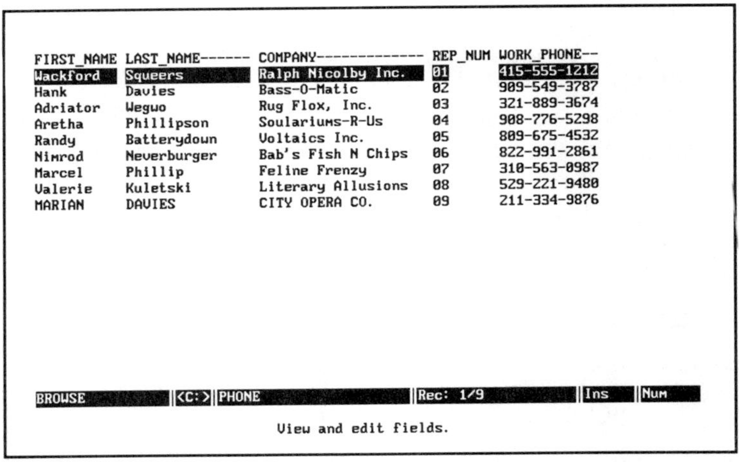

FIRST_NAME	LAST_NAME------	COMPANY-------------	REP_NUM	WORK_PHONE--
Wackford	Squeers	Ralph Nicolby Inc.	01	415-555-1212
Hank	Davies	Bass-O-Matic	02	909-549-3787
Adriator	Weguo	Rug Flox, Inc.	03	321-889-3674
Aretha	Phillipson	Soulariums-R-Us	04	908-776-5298
Randy	Batterydown	Voltaics Inc.	05	809-675-4532
Nimrod	Neverburger	Bab's Fish N Chips	06	822-991-2861
Marcel	Phillip	Feline Frenzy	07	310-563-0987
Valerie	Kuletski	Literary Allusions	08	529-221-9480
MARIAN	DAVIES	CITY OPERA CO.	09	211-334-9876

BROWSE ‖<C:>‖PHONE ‖Rec: 1/9 ‖Ins ‖Num

View and edit fields.

■ *Figure 17.1: A linking field is added to PHONE*

STEP 17

Opening the Files for the View

Next you need to create the View that connects the databases and determines which fields are linked and which fields will display.

1. Open the appropriate databases. Select Create/View.
2. Choose the disk drive on which your databases are stored.
3. Type in a name for the View. In this case, call it **REP**.
4. A new screen appears, displaying five menu options. This is the Create View screen, where you create your multifile View. The first menu, Set Up, shows a list of database files. Just select the files you want in the View by highlighting them one at a time and pressing Enter. A little arrow appears to the left of each file name you've selected. Each time you press Enter for each database, the Index box will appear. Typically you'll only have to select an index for the linked file (in our example, the PHONE database) unless you also want the master file (STEREO) indexed for easier access.

Arrow means file is selected

CATEGORY--	BRAND-----	MODEL-	QUANTITY	WHOLESALE	LAST_ORDER	REP_NUM
RECEIVER	NIZO	T-33	5	225.49	05/15/92	02
RECEIVER	NIZO	T-35	4	312.00	01/12/92	02
RECEIVER	ACME	R25-MT	13	19.99	01/12/92	09
RECEIVER	NADIR	Z-CHP	50	12.95	03/06/53	01
SPEAKERS	RAZCO	L-55	30	199.00	07/13/92	03
SPEAKERS	TALBEST	BG-20	6	250.00	03/01/91	04
TAPE DECK	ROLLEM	CAS-3	10	125.65	09/15/92	03
TAPE DECK	FLOWUTTER	WBL-5	5	149.33	09/01/92	05
TURNTABLE	XIRTAM	Z5-L	5	99.99	10/01/92	06
TURNTABLE	RALURIC	RND-1	3	595.00	02/28/90	07
TELEVISION	BLABBEX	KZZ	29	189.99	/ /	08
TELEVISION	BIG-VUE	BV-45	5	595.00	/ /	09
VCR	CINOSANAP	TP-120	3	540.99	/ /	03
VIDEO TAPE	MAXWELL	XX-120	45	3.49	/ /	05
VCR	THINEX	TV-29	14	149.00	/ /	07

BROWSE | <C:> | STEREO | Rec: 15/15 | Ins | Num

View and edit fields.

▪ *Figure 17.2: A linking field is added to STEREO*

STEP 17

Setting Up the Relationship for the View

Now you need to tell dBASE which file is the master file and which file or files are to be linked. Remember, the master file is the one that controls the show. For our example, we want the STEREO database to be the master file and PHONE to be the linked file.

1. Press ← to leave the Index box.
2. Type **R** to select the Relate menu.
3. The databases you selected earlier appear in a box. The program wants to know which is the master file, or as the Message Line says, which one is "the file that will initiate the relation." Choose STEREO.
4. A new box appears showing the other file name(s) and the message

   ```
   Select the database file that will accept
   the relation.
   ```

   Choose PHONE. The little arrow appears to the right of the file name. The Message Line reads

   ```
   Enter an expression
   The master key expression is REP_NUM.
   ```

   Basically, dBASE needs you to specify which index you're using to link the two databases, and is reminding you that PHONE is indexed on REP_NUM. You can type in the name **REP_NUM**, or press F10 and choose the index from a list of index files on disk. The screen in Figure 17.3 illustrates this step.
5. Press Enter to accept the index, then → once or twice to exit the Relate menu and open the Fields menu.

Selecting the Fields List

Now you have to select the fields you want displayed in the View. Remember that you'll have at least twice as many fields as you're used to working with at once. Of course, you can see them all if you

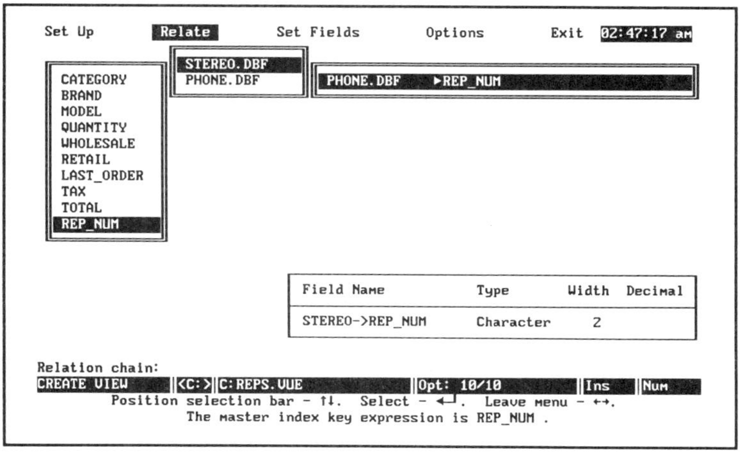

▪ ***Figure 17.3: Setting the Master index***

want, but this can be messy. It's best to keep things simple, if possible. In this case, I'll reduce the Fields list so that I can get everything I want on the screen at one time.

1. Choose the first database and press Enter.
2. A Fields list for that database appears. Little arrows are next to each field, meaning that all fields are selected as a default. Turn off the ones you don't want by highlighting them and pressing Enter. I've left on BRAND, MODEL, and QUANTITY from the STEREO database.
3. Next, leave that menu with →.
4. Select PHONE from the database list. Keep FIRST_NAME, LAST_NAME, and WORK_PHONE for the View.
5. Press → to leave the Set Fields menu.
6. Save the View by selecting Exit/Save.

STEP 17

Enjoying the View

To use the View, follow the steps below.

1. Select Set Up/View.
2. Choose the drive and the View file name (in this case, REP.VUE).
3. Select Retrieve/List/Execute the Command. The results are shown in Figure 17.4.

Note how easy it is now to check your current inventory quantities and locate the name and number of the appropriate reps so you can order more items.

OTHER VIEW OPTIONS

Browse and Edit use View too

You can use Browse and Edit with the active View. You can also create a report utilizing any of the fields in the View.

There is another View option that you should consider. The Options menu on the View screen lets you set up a condition on your View so

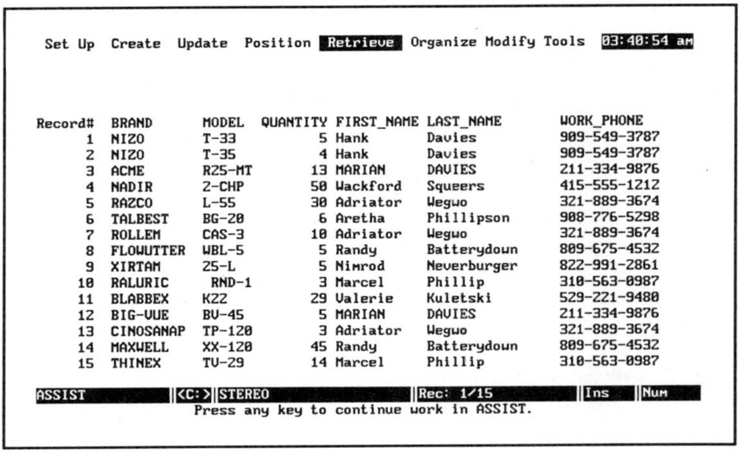

Set Up Create Update Position Retrieve Organize Modify Tools 03:40:54 am

Record#	BRAND	MODEL	QUANTITY	FIRST_NAME	LAST_NAME	WORK_PHONE
1	NIZO	T-33	5	Hank	Davies	909-549-3787
2	NIZO	T-35	4	Hank	Davies	909-549-3787
3	ACME	RZ5-MT	13	MARIAN	DAVIES	211-334-9876
4	NADIR	Z-CHP	50	Wackford	Squeers	415-555-1212
5	RAZCO	L-55	30	Adriator	Weguo	321-889-3674
6	TALBEST	BG-20	6	Aretha	Phillipson	908-776-5298
7	ROLLEM	CAS-3	10	Adriator	Weguo	321-889-3674
8	FLOWUTTER	WBL-5	5	Randy	Batterydown	809-675-4532
9	XIRTAM	Z5-L	5	Nimrod	Neverburger	822-991-2861
10	RALURIC	RND-1	3	Marcel	Phillip	310-563-0987
11	BLABBEX	KZZ	29	Valerie	Kuletski	529-221-9480
12	BIG-VUE	BV-45	5	MARIAN	DAVIES	211-334-9876
13	CINOSANAP	TP-120	3	Adriator	Weguo	321-889-3674
14	MAXWELL	XX-120	45	Randy	Batterydown	809-675-4532
15	THINEX	TV-29	14	Marcel	Phillip	310-563-0987

ASSIST <C:> STEREO Rec: 1/15 Ins Num

Press any key to continue work in ASSIST.

▪ *Figure 17.4: The linked View*

that only certain records are displayed. For example, suppose you want to show only those items where the quantity is lower than five, so that you can reorder them.

1. Select Modify/View and choose REP.VUE as the file name.
2. Select Options/Filter.
3. Press F10. A Fields list appears.
4. Highlight QUANTITY. The Message Line reads

   Enter a logical expression to filter the records in this View.

5. Press Enter. Finish the filter expression in the Filter box by typing <5.
6. Save the View.
7. List the data again. Now only three records show up, as you see in Figure 17.5.

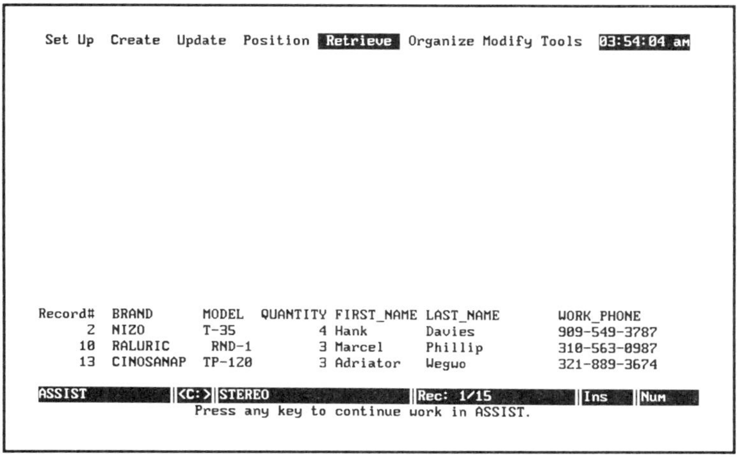

▪ *Figure 17.5: Applying a filter to the View*

VIEW TIPS

Here are some important points to remember when creating views:

- You may have as many as 15 databases linked in any given View.
- Each file is linked to the next one in the chain by one (and only one) field. The linkage is declared in the same manner explained earlier in this Step.
- The two fields used for each linkage must have the same name, type, width, and contents.
- When linking more than two files in a chain, remember that any given file can be linked "into" only once. In our example, PHONE was linked "into" STEREO. If you wanted to add another database to this view, it would have to link into PHONE, not STEREO.
- Linked files should each have the same number of records to work properly.
- Each file must contain corresponding records for each entry in the common field. In our case, all rep numbers appearing in the master file, STEREO, needed a matching record in the linked database, PHONE.
- Finally, to turn off a View, you can quit dBASE and start it up again, run another View via the Set Up menu, or go to the dot prompt and type

  ```
  CLEAR ALL
  ```

If you intend to go directly to the next Step, turn off the View in one of the ways described above.

Updating One File from Another

The last two Steps have explained a few ways to use multiple databases simultaneously. This Step covers one of the most powerful applications for multiple databases—automatically updating one database from another. A word of caution, however: this is a rather complex undertaking, so if updating in this way isn't something you plan to do often, you might want to skip this Step and jump ahead to Step 19.

USING THE UPDATE COMMAND

Rather than simply adding records to a master file from a related file, as you did with the Append command in Step 16, more complex business applications often call for updating master file data with information from an associated database. The Update command (not to be confused with the Update menu in the Assistant) lets you do this.

Consider this example. Suppose we want to have a computer in the receiving room of the stereo store. Then, as new shipments of equipment arrive by truck, a person in the receiving room could enter the part and serial numbers of the items into a separate database. At the end of the day, we could update the QUANTITY field in the STEREO database from the receiving list in one fell swoop, reflecting all the receipts of the day.

Of course, we could use the STEREO database in the receiving room and let the employee working there update the inventory, avoiding the need for a new database. But there's a hitch—the serial numbers. Each individual piece received needs a separate record, even if the item is of the same type as another item, to hold the item's unique serial number. In the STEREO database, there is only one record for each item *type;* we can't list each Acme receiver and its serial number (which we need for warranty purposes) separately. The STEREO database was structured in this way because it was more useful to consolidate all the equipment of the same brand and model into a single quantity. If we record the serial numbers in a second database, we can use the Update command to update the STEREO database's QUANTITY field while retaining the advantages of the STEREO database structure.

1. First, we need to create a link between the two databases we wish to use. This time, we'll use the part number as the link. Begin by adding a new field to the STEREO database. In this case, we'll add a Character field 3 letters wide. The field data is shown in Figure 18.1. (I've used the Set Fields command to limit the number of fields displayed.)

2. Next, create the receiving list database, called RECV. It has two fields and looks like this:

Field	Field Name	Type	Width	Dec
1	PART	Character	3	
2	SERIAL_NUM	Character	6	

   Fill it with the data shown in Figure 18.2 to simulate a list of items received for the day.

Indexing on the linking field

Recall that when you linked databases in a View you had to index the second (linked) file on the linking field. To use the Update command, you must index the master file instead. If the update database is huge, you might want to index the linked file too (on the same field), but it's not necessary.

Note that updating of this nature has to be done from the dot prompt.

1. Index STEREO on the PART field by typing in the following commands. Press Enter after each line.

   SELECT 1

   USE STEREO

```
. set fields to category, brand, model, quantity, rep_num, part
. list
Record#  CATEGORY   BRAND      MODEL   QUANTITY REP_NUM PART
      1  RECEIVER   NIZO       T-33           5 02      001
      2  RECEIVER   NIZO       T-35           4 02      002
      3  RECEIVER   ACME       R25-MT        13 09      005
      4  RECEIVER   NADIR      Z-CHP         50 01      007
      5  SPEAKERS   RAZCO      L-55          30 03      008
      6  SPEAKERS   TALBEST    BG-20          6 04      010
      7  TAPE DECK  ROLLEM     CAS-3         10 03      004
      8  TAPE DECK  FLOWUTTER  WBL-5          5 05      003
      9  TURNTABLE  XIRTAM     25-L           5 06      011
     10  TURNTABLE  RALURIC    RND-1          3 07      009
     11  TELEVISION BLABBEX    K22           29 08      006
     12  TELEVISION BIG-VUE    BV-45          5 09      012
     13  VCR        CINOSANAP  TP-120         3 03      014
     14  VIDEO TAPE MAXWELL    XX-120        45 05      013
     15  VCR        THINEX     TV-29         14 07      015

.
.
Command Line  ||<C:>||STEREO              ||Rec: EOF/15          ||      ||Num
                       Enter a dBASE III PLUS command.
```

■ *Figure 18.1: The PART field added to STEREO*

```
. list
Record#  PART SERIAL_NUM
      1  001  234595
      2  001  234958
      3  005  9943-t
      4  012  555554
      5  004  100022
      6  005  399990
      7  008  495891
      8  010  111223
.
Command Line  ||<C:>||RECV                ||Rec: EOF/8           ||Ins   ||Num
                       Enter a dBASE III PLUS command.
```

■ *Figure 18.2: Data for the RECV file*

```
INDEX ON PART TO PARTNUM [Enter]
SET INDEX TO PARTNUM [Enter]
```

2. Open the RECV database in workarea 2 by entering

```
SELECT 2
USE RECV
```

3. Select workarea 1 again—this is the information you want to update.

```
SELECT 1 [Enter]
```

Here's how the update works. The Update command tells dBASE to go though the RECV file, look at each record, and determine what is the part number of each new item. Then the program looks through the STEREO database to find the record that has the matching part number. When the appropriate record is found in the STEREO file, dBASE increases the number in its QUANTITY field by 1.

Executing the Update command

4. Type in the command

```
UPDATE ON PART FROM RECV REPLACE QUANTITY
WITH QUANTITY+1 RANDOM
```

Figure 18.3 shows the result. Note that the QUANTITY field has been updated appropriately. The "random" part of the command is necessary only because we didn't index the RECV database on the update key field, PART.

Feeling lost?

If you feel a little lost with this command, don't worry. It's one of the most complex commands in dBASE III PLUS. If you're baffled, it may help to divide our sample command into two parts, with capitalization changed and with the words you fill in shown in italics, for clarity.

UPDATE on *PART* from *RECV* REPLACE *QUANTITY* with *QUANTITY+1* random

The first half of the command says: "Update the current file from the RECV file, using the index key field, PART. (A key field is the field on which the database is currently indexed.) The second half

```
. list
Record#  CATEGORY   BRAND      MODEL  QUANTITY PART
      1  RECEIVER   NIZO       T-33          7 001
      2  RECEIVER   NIZO       T-35          4 002
      8  TAPE DECK  FLOWUTTER  WBL-5         5 003
      7  TAPE DECK  ROLLEM     CAS-3        11 004
      3  RECEIVER   ACME       R25-MT       15 005
     11  TELEVISION BLABBEX    K22          29 006
      4  RECEIVER   NADIR      Z-CHP        50 007
      5  SPEAKERS   RAZCO      L-55         31 008
     10  TURNTABLE  RALURIC    RND-1         3 009
      6  SPEAKERS   TALBEST    BG-20         7 010
      9  TURNTABLE  XIRTAM     Z5-L          5 011
     12  TELEVISION BIG-VUE    BV-45         6 012
     14  VIDEO TAPE MAXWELL    XX-120       45 013
     13  VCR        CINOSANAP  TP-120        3 014
     15  VCR        THINEX     TV-29        14 015
.
Command Line  ||<C:>||STEREO          ||Rec: EOF/15        ||Ins  ||Num

                   Enter a dBASE III PLUS command.
```

■ ***Figure 18.3: The result of the Update command***

says: "Each time you find a match between the part numbers in the two files, add 1 to the QUANTITY field in the master file, and by the way, the From database isn't indexed."

UPDATING TIPS

Here are some points to remember when updating:

- The database you are modifying via the Update command must be open and in the currently selected workarea. The file must be either indexed or sorted on the field that links the two files.
- The other database (called the "From" database) must meet three requirements:
  1. It must have the key field in common with the To database (same name, size, and type).
  2. If the From database isn't sorted or indexed, the word *random* must be included at the end of the Update command.
  3. The From file must be open in an unselected workarea.

45

Custom Data-Entry Screens

This Step shows you how to create your own data-entry and editing screens.

Up to now you've worked with your data using the format that dBASE provides. For example, when Appending, Browsing and Editing, you pretty much have to take the positions of fields as they come. It's pretty primitive, especially when Appending and Editing. Fields are stacked up on one another in the same order in which they were entered when you created the structure. Even worse, those cryptic field names, limited to eight characters, could confuse data-entry people and cause errors in input.

Fields anywhere on screen

However, you don't have to settle for the supplied arrangement. dBASE has a built-in feature called the Screen Painter with which you can create customized format screens for data entry and display. Fields can be placed anywhere on the screen, with instructions and prompts written around them, using field descriptions of your choice. You may even want to create a screen that looks very much like the paper forms you used before computerizing.

With the Screen Painter you can also elect to have dBASE do range checking for you, to decrease data-entry mistakes.

STEP 19

As an example, we're going to create the data entry and lookup screen for the Stereo database shown in Figure 19.1. However, I'm going to give you instructions that are sufficiently general for use with any database.

OK. Here's how to do it.

STARTING A NEW SCREEN

1. Choose Create/Format.
2. Select the drive and then type in the name you want to assign to the screen. The program adds an *.SCR* extension for you.
3. The Screen Painter Main menu appears, with the Select Database File highlighted. Press Enter and select the database file for which you want a custom data-entry screen.
4. Nothing appears to happen. Now select Load Fields. Choose the fields you want on the data screen by highlighting them and pressing Enter. The little arrow appears next to those you've selected. You see, you don't have to include all the fields. This is an effective way to eliminate access to

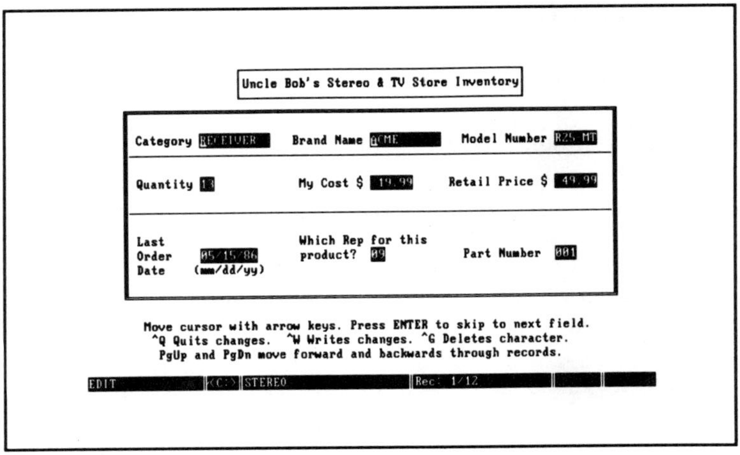

▪ ***Figure 19.1: The final data-entry screen***

sensitive fields in your database. For our example, I've chosen CATEGORY, BRAND, MODEL, QUANTITY, WHOLESALE, RETAIL, LAST_ORDER, REP_NUM, and PART.

5. Press → to leave the box. The fields are placed on the screen, but notice how odd they look. Character fields have Xs in them and numeric fields have 9s. Date fields display 9s with slash (/) marks between them. Don't worry—these are just place holders and indicate the format of each field. You can alter these, as I'll explain later.

Now you're ready to position the fields on the screen at the desired locations and to add the boxes, lines, and prompts.

Moving the Fields Around

Now you have to drag the fields to their desired locations. Note the editing keys in Table 19.1. You'll use them while painting.

Main Key	*Letter Key*	*Action*
Moving		
→ ← ↑ ↓		Moves the cursor in the indicated direction.
End	^F	Moves to the next word.
Home	^A	Moves to the previous word.
Enter		Moves down a line. Inserts a line if insert is on.
PgDn	^C	Moves the cursor up 18 lines.
PgUp	^R	Moves the cursor down 18 lines.
Deleting		
Del	^G	Deletes letter at cursor position.
Backspace		Deletes letter left of cursor.

Table 19.1: Screen design editing keys

Main Key	Letter Key	Action
^T		Deletes letters to end of word.
^Y		Deletes the line the cursor is on.
^U		Deletes the field or box the cursor is on.
Inserting		
Ins	^V	Toggles insert mode on/off.
^N		Inserts blank line at cursor.
Other		
F10		Switches between blackboard and menu mode.

Table 19.1: Screen design editing keys (continued)

But first a word of warning. If you press the Ins key or ^V while the cursor is positioned on a field, you will change the field's length just as if you had altered it on the Modify Structure screen. This isn't a great idea, because you could lose data. The Del key does the same, so be cautious with these keys.

To position the fields, you do the following:

1. Move the cursor so that it's positioned on the field that you want to move (the part with the 9s or the Xs). Then press Enter. The field jumps to the new location. Note that the field name stays put, so it's easy to lose track of which field is which. Notice though, that when you put the cursor on a field, its identity is revealed at the bottom of the screen. The database file name precedes the field name like this:

   ```
   STEREO ->CATEGORY
   ```

   so you can identify it later.

2. Move the rest of the fields around to positions that suit you. Keep your eye on the Navigation and Message lines. They will tell you exactly how to move things around.

Notice the Status Line. It has a section that reports the coordinates of the cursor while it is on the "blackboard." (The blackboard is the work area in which you are painting your screen.) Using the coordinates will help you to line up fields on the screen.

3. Now you can name the fields with prompts that suit you, prompts that will convey more meaning than the cryptic, actual field names in the database's structure.

4. If you find that your spacing is too tight or loose, vertically speaking, you can add or subtract blank lines easily with ^N or ^Y.

5. Eliminate the old field names either by turning off Insert mode and typing spaces over them, or by putting the cursor on their first letter and pressing ^T. (Note that the latter technique tends to pull things left on the screen, which can be irritating.)

Adding Boxes

Now you can add boxes to your screen, spiffing them up nicely, or to separate sections of related data fields for easier recognition. Here's how:

1. Press F10. Choose Options/Double Bar.

2. Move the cursor to the upper left corner of the desired box location, and press Enter.

3. Move the cursor to the position where you want the lower right corner of the box, and press Enter.

You can alter the box's size after it is drawn. Place the cursor on the side you want to pull or push and press Enter. Then use the arrow keys to resize, and press Enter when you're through.

To draw a vertical or horizontal line (rather than a box), you just draw a "box" with no width, or no height. Note that you can also draw single lines.

Saving and Using the File

To save your file and use it:

1. Press F10 and select Exit/Save.
2. The Assistant returns. Select Set Up/Format for Screen. Select the drive and format file (STEREO.FMT in the example). The Set Up menu reappears. It looks as if nothing has happened. Actually, something has.
3. Make sure the desired database is open. Then select Update/Edit. Record number 1 should appear in your new screen arrangement.

ADDING RANGE CHECKING AND PICTURE TEMPLATES

Just as with all other types of files in dBASE, you can modify your custom screen after you've created it. So, if you have second thoughts, just select Modify/Format from the Assistant, open the correct file, and go back to work. Here are the steps for adding Range Checking to a screen, whether it's the first time around or an afterthought.

Range Checking

Range checking can be added to a custom format screen for a variety of purposes. Typically, it is added to prevent invalid data such as erroneous dates from being entered. However, range checking can be done only for Numeric and Date fields.

Here are the steps for adding range checking to a field.

1. Place the cursor on the field for which you want range checking.
2. Press F10.
3. The field definition for the field pops up in a box.
4. Select Range.

5. Another smaller box will appear asking what the upper and lower limits of the range should be. Select Lower.
6. The familiar arrow appears. Type in the lower limit of the range checking. If it's a date field you're working with, the slashes will have been filled in for you.
7. Press Enter and then the ↓, and then press Enter again, to input the upper limit.
8. Press ← to leave the menu, then F10 to return to your screen.

Using the Picture Template

Picture Template is another choice from the Screen Painter's Options menu. It lets you format Character fields in a number of ways. By default, the Screen Painter fills all character fields with Xs. (These Xs don't appear when you actually use the screen; they indicate which types of letters or numbers will be accepted into a field.) You can change the acceptable "picture template" for a field by changing the Xs to any of the following codes:

Symbol	*Effect*
A	Allows entry of letters only.
L	Allows entry of T,F,Y, or N.
N	Allows entry of letters and numbers only.
X	Allows entry of any characters (letters, numbers, punctuation marks, etc.).
Y	Allows entry of Y or N only.
#	Allows entry of numbers, spaces, periods, and + or - signs only.
9	Allows entry of numbers and + or - signs only.
!	Allows any characters; converts all letters to uppercase.

1. On the screen you're designing, highlight the field whose template you want to alter.
2. Press F10. Choose Options/Picture Template.
3. Type in the template you want to use, referring to the help box that lists the types. For example, for a Character field with a width of 10, you could type in !!!!!!!!!! to allow entry of any characters and to convert all letters to uppercase as they're entered.
4. Press F10 to return to your screen.

There is another kind of format option which can make life easier for data-entry people. You can specify certain characters to be inserted automatically in the fields of each new record you append. For example, typing in the parentheses or dashes as punctuation when entering zillions of phone numbers is bothersome. Using the picture

```
###-###-####
```

in the template for a phone number field eliminates the need to type the punctuation each time you add a record.

Display Only Fields

Sometimes you may want certain fields to be "display only." This will prevent anyone from altering the contents of certain fields while editing. You do this from the Screen Painter's Modify menu.

1. Put the cursor on the field that you want to render "display only."
2. Press F10. Select Modify/Action and press Enter. The highlighted words next to Action change Edit/GET to Display/SAY. Then press F10 to return to the Blackboard. Repeat this process for each field that you want to change to display only. Then save the new form.

15

Importing and Exporting Files

In this Step you'll learn how to import and export data between dBASE and other popular programs and file formats.

Hundreds of thousands of databases are created using programs other than dBASE. It's not unlikely that at some point you'll have to import a foreign database file into dBASE, or export a file to another program. Luckily, dBASE is such a standard in the microcomputer industry that many programs are designed with the capability to read and write files in dBASE format.

Other programs supported

The dBASE program supports the many database and wordprocessing programs that create and use ASCII (American Standard Code for Information Interchange) database files. The program also has a built-in converter for importing files from other, non-ASCII, programs. These compatible programs are listed below.

File	*Extension*
PFS:FILE	.PFS
Lotus 1-2-3 Spreadsheet	.WKS
Multiplan Spreadshee	.SYLK
VisiCalc	.DIF

Importing ASCII Files

You can import from ASCII files of two formats:

ASCII Format	*Type*	*Description of Source File*
Delimited	DELIMITED	Fields are separated by commas or blanks. Delimiters such as " (double quotes) enclose Character fields.
System Data Format	SDF	Fields are of fixed length and a carriage return and line feed separate records.

Typical delimited files are those from Wordstar MailMerge ™ and sequential access database files created in BASIC. The SDF files include databases created by FORTRAN programs, usually on mainframe business computers.

To import one of these types of files:

1. Create a new dBASE database with a structure based on your knowledge of the source file. Determine the exact length of each field and how the fields are delimited, if at all.
2. From the dot prompt, use the command

   APPEND FROM *SOURCE FILENAME* TYPE SDF

   to import an SDF file. To import a delimited file, type

   APPEND FROM *SOURCE FILENAME* TYPE DELIMITED [WITH *DELIMITER*]

These commands are rather esoteric and won't be used that often. Note that the second form of the command requires you to specify the delimiter, if it is other than double quote marks. For example,

```
APPEND FROM CONTACTS TYPE DELIMITED WITH ¦
```

could be altered to use double quotes as delimiters:

```
APPEND FROM CONTACTS TYPE DELIMITED
```

IMPORTING NON-ASCII FILES

PFS files

There is a converter option in dBASE that makes importing PFS files very easy. The converter option accomplishes this by separating the imported PFS file into three new dBASE files with the extensions .DBF, .FMT, and .VUE. (These files are given the same first name as the PFS file.) The .FMT file formats the screen in the same way PFS:FILE did. Thus, your database screen will look the same in dBASE as it did in PFS. To import a PFS:FILE database to dBASE III PLUS follow the steps below.

1. Select Tools/Import.
2. Choose the drive name and the name of the file you want to import. The file name must include any extensions. (PFS files rarely have extensions, however.)
3. Press Enter.

The new files are created. If you have a catalog open, the new files are entered into the catalog. (A catalog is a collection of related files such as a database, view, report, and label files. By organizing files into a catalog, you can more easily keep track of those that are used together. See the dBASE manual for more information about catalogs.) Whenever you open the database from the catalog, the screen format (.FMT) file will be opened automatically. If you're not using a catalog, open the file with the Set Up/View command from the Assistant or type at the dot prompt

```
SET VIEW TO [FILENAME]
```

and fill in the name of the .VUE file that was created during the importing process.

Importing from WKS, SYLK, and DIF

To import files from programs other than PFS, you have to use another approach.

1. Create a file with the approximate structure you want. The order of the fields, as well as field sizes and types, should match those of the file you want to import. For spreadsheet files, each row in the spreadsheet becomes a record in the database; each column supplies the data for a single field. Be sure that your database field sizes match the spreadsheet cell sizes.
2. Open the new database. At the dot prompt, type in the command

   APPEND FROM *FILENAME* TYPE *FILE TYPE*

   where *filename* is the complete name of the source file, and *file type* is WKS, SYLK, or DIF. The dBASE program will import the records, then report the number of records appended to your database.
3. Examine the contents of the file, using Browse or List. If fields are too long or short, you may want to adjust the size of the fields and try again.

EXPORTING FILES

You can export as many types of files as you can import. All the logic and rules explained above apply. Only the actual command names differ.

Exporting PFS

To turn a dBASE file into a PFS file,

1. Open the dBASE file (and screen format or View if you wish these to be reflected in the PFS file).

2. Choose Tools/Export from the Assistant.
3. Enter the drive and file name.

If you didn't open a format (*.FMT*) file, the default dBASE III PLUS file structure becomes the PFS screen format.

Exporting to WKS, SYLK, DIF

To export to these formats, you use the general approach described in the import section. However, you must use a different command from the dot prompt. In place of Append, use Copy.

1. Open the database you want to copy from.
2. From the dot prompt type:

   ```
   COPY TO DESTINATION FILENAME TYPE
   [WKS, SYLK, DIF]
   ```

   For example, to create a WKS file from the STEREO database, first open the STEREO database, then type:

   ```
   COPY TO STEREO.WKS TYPE WKS
   ```

Exporting to ASCII

If you want an ASCII text file created out of a database file, it's a fairly simple process. You might want to do this to desktop publish a phone directory or other listing, or just to import a listing into a word processing document.

1. Open the source database.
2. From the dot prompt, type

   ```
   COPY TO DESTINATION FILENAME SDF
   ```

This creates an SDF text file, with fields laid out in columns. The file below was created using this command and imported into my word processing file in PC-Write, for this book.

Wackford	Squeers	Ralph Nicolby Inc.
Hank	Davies	Bass-O-Matic
Adriator	Wegwo	Rug Flox, Inc.
Aretha	Phillipson	Soulariums-R-Us
Randy	Batterydown	Voltaics Inc.
Nimrod	Neverburger	Bab's Fish N Chips
Marcel	Phillip	Feline Frenzy
Valerie	Kuletski	Literary Allusions
MARIAN	DAVIES	CITY OPERA CO.

If you want to delimit the fields, that is done with the delimiter option. Basically, the command looks like this:

COPY TO *DESTINATION FILENAME* TYPE DELIMITED

```
"Wackford","Squeers","Ralph Nicolby Inc."
"Hank","Davies","Bass-O-Matic"
"Adriator","Wegwo","Rug Flox, Inc."
"Aretha","Phillipson","Soulariums-R-Us"
"Randy","Batterydown","Voltaics Inc."
"Nimrod","Neverburger","Bab's Fish N Chips"
"Marcel","Phillip","Feline Frenzy"
"Valerie","Kuletski","Literary Allusions"
"MARIAN","DAVIES","CITY OPERA CO."
```

Just as with importing, you can change the delimiters by adding the "with [*delimiter*]" at the end of the command. If you want blanks to delimit the fields, use the command

COPY TO *DESTINATION FILENAME* TYPE
DELIMITED WITH BLANK

Here's the resulting ASCII file:

Wackford Squeers Ralph Nicolby Inc.

Hank Davies Bass-O-Matic

Adriator Wegwo Rug Flox, Inc.

Aretha Phillipson Soulariums-R-Us

Randy Batterydown Voltaics Inc.

Nimrod Neverburger Bab's Fish N Chips

Marcel Phillip Feline Frenzy

Valerie Kuletski Literary Allusions

MARIAN DAVIES CITY OPERA CO.

A

B

C

D

E

F

G

H

I

T

U

V

W

Y

Z

Selections from The SYBEX Library

DATABASES

The ABC's of dBASE III PLUS
Robert Cowart
264pp. Ref. 379-1
The most efficient way to get beginners up and running with dBASE. Every 'how' and 'why' of database management is demonstrated through tutorials and practical dBASE III PLUS applications.

The ABC's of dBASE IV 1.1
Robert Cowart
350pp, Ref. 632-4
The latest version of dBASE IV is featured in this hands-on introduction. It assumes no previous experience with computers or database management, and uses easy-to-follow lessons to introduce the concepts, build basic skills, and set up some practical applications. Includes report writing and Query by Example.

The ABC's of FoxPro
Scott D. Palmer
296pp. Ref. 705-3
A step-by-step introduction to database management with FoxPro. Readers set up and work with a customer file, sort and index records, design and print reports, produce form letters and mailing labels, and link two data files. Includes a preview of FoxPro's advanced features.

The ABC's of Paradox 3.5 (Second Edition)
Charles Siegel
334pp, Ref. 785-1
This easy-to-follow, hands-on tutorial is a must for beginning users of Paradox 3.0 and 3.5. Even if you've never used a computer before, you'll be doing useful work in just a few short lessons. A clear introduction to database management and valuable business examples make this a "right-to-work" guide for the practical-minded.

The ABC's of Quattro Pro 2
Alan Simpson
Douglas J. Wolf
338pp. Ref. 754-1
Even if you've never used a computer before, this book will have you using Quattro Pro more quickly than you dreamed possible. Learn to install and start up the program; build your first business spreadsheet; edit and organize data to suit your needs; use formulas and functions, and much more.

Advanced Techniques in dBASE III PLUS
Alan Simpson
454pp. Ref. 369-4
A full course in database design and structured programming, with routines for inventory control, accounts receivable, system management, and integrated databases.

dBASE Instant Reference SYBEX Prompter Series
Alan Simpson
471pp. Ref. 484-4
Comprehensive information at a glance: a brief explanation of syntax and usage for every dBASE command, with step-by-step instructions and exact keystroke sequences. Commands are grouped by function in twenty precise categories.

dBASE III PLUS Programmer's Reference Guide SYBEX Ready Reference Series
Alan Simpson
1056pp. Ref. 508-5
Programmers will save untold hours and effort using this comprehensive, well-organized dBASE encyclopedia. Com-

plete technical details on commands and functions, plus scores of often-needed algorithms.

dBASE IV 1.1 Programmer's Desktop Reference

Alan Simpson

1050pp. Ref. 539-5

This comprehensive seven-part reference is a must for dBASE programmers. It offers full details on every command and function, as well as practical techniques and algorithms for achieving specific programming goals. Fully cross-referenced and indexed by command, function, and topic.

dBASE IV 1.1 Programmer's Instant Reference (Second Edition)

Alan Simpson

555pp, Ref. 764-9

Enjoy fast, easy access to information often hidden in cumbersome documentation. This handy pocket-sized reference presents information on each command and function in the dBASE IV programming language. Commands are grouped according to their purpose, so readers can locate the correct command for any task—quickly and easily.

dBASE IV User's Instant Reference (Second Edition)

Alan Simpson

356pp, Ref. 786-X

Completely revised to cover the new 1.1 version of dBASE IV, this handy reference guide presents information on every dBASE operation a user can perform. Exact keystroke sequences are presented, and complex tasks are explained step-by-step. It's a great way for newer users to look up the basics, while more experienced users will find it a fast way to locate information on specialized tasks.

Mastering DataEase

Susan Harmon

531pp. Ref. 689-8

A thorough, hands-on introduction to database management with DataEase, stressing skills for on-the-job productivity. Build a sample inventory management system, while mastering quick reporting, custom form design, multi-file applications, using Data Query Language, and system maintenance.

Mastering dBASE III PLUS: A Structured Approach

Carl Townsend

342pp. Ref. 372-4

In-depth treatment of structured programming for custom dBASE solutions. An ideal study and reference guide for applications developers, new and experienced users with an interest in efficient programming.

Mastering dBASE IV 1.1 Programming

Carl Townsend

546pp. Ref. 782-9

An in-depth introduction especially for applications developers, and for experienced dBASE users seeking programming skills. This up-to-date new edition covers 1.1 basics, structured programming and database design, and specific techniques for business application programming—with examples for general ledger and invoicing.

Mastering FoxPro

Charles Seigel

639pp. Ref. 671-5

This guide to the powerful FoxPro DBMS offers a tutorial on database basics, then enables the reader to master new skills and features as needed—with many examples from business. An in-depth tutorial guides users through the development of a complete mailing list system.

Mastering Paradox 3.5

Alan Simpson

650pp, Ref. 677-4

This indispensable, in-depth guide has again been updated for the latest Paradox release, offering the same comprehensive, hands-on treatment featured in highly praised previous editions. It covers everything from database basics to PAL programming—including complex queries and reports, and multi-table applications.

Mastering Q&A (Second Edition)

Greg Harvey

540pp. Ref. 452-6

This hands-on tutorial explores the Q&A Write, File, and Report modules, and the Intelligent Assistant. English-language command processor, macro creation, interfacing with other software, and more, using practical business examples.

Mastering Q&A 4

Alan R. Neibauer

500pp. Ref. 735-5

This hands-on guide is now covering the latest Q&A release. Tutorials and sample applications illustrate every aspect of using Q&A: treating and manipulating data bases, printing reports, multi-file applications and look-up tables, and integrating Q&A with Lotus 1-2-3; plus networking, macros, and programming the IA. Special sections for word processing and generating form letters and labels.

Paradox 3.5 User's Instant Reference

Loy Anderson
Cary Jensen

186pp. Ref. 766-5

Quick access to concise information on every feature of Paradox 3.0 and 3.5. Entries are organized by function, and provide exact keystrokes, command options, instructions for common tasks, and thorough cross-references. Topics include creating and working with tables; forms; reports; queries; crosstabs; graphs; tools; scripts and PAL; networking; and SQL.

Understanding dBASE III

Alan Simpson

300pp. Ref. 267-1

dBASE commands and concepts are illustrated throughout with practical, business oriented examples—for mailing list handling, accounts receivable, and inventory design. Contains scores of tips and techniques for maximizing efficiency and meeting special needs.

Understanding dBASE III PLUS

Alan Simpson

415pp. Ref. 349-X

A solid sourcebook of training and ongoing support. Everything from creating a first database to command file programming is presented in working examples, with tips and techniques you won't find anywhere else.

Understanding dBASE IV 1.1

Alan Simpson

900pp, Ref. 633-2

Simpson's outstanding introduction to dBASE—brought up to date for version 1.1—uses tutorials and practical examples to build effective, and increasingly sophisticated, database management skills. Advanced topics include custom reporting, managing multiple databases, and designing custom applications.

Understanding Oracle

James T. Perry
Joseph G. Lateer

634pp. Ref. 534-4

A comprehensive guide to the Oracle database management system for administrators, users, and applications developers. Covers everything in Version 5 from database basics to multi-user systems, performance, and development tools including SQL*Forms, SQL*Report, and SQL*Calc. Includes Fast Track speed notes.

Understanding Professional File

Gerry Litton

463pp. Re. 669-3

Build practical data management skills in an orderly fashion with this complete step-by-step tutorial—from creating a simple database to building customized business applications.

Retrieving Information

Purpose	Assistant Commands	Dot Prompt Command
List all records	Retrieve/List	LIST
Show current record or groups of records	Update/Display *or* Retrieve/Display	DISPLAY
Run report	Retrieve/Report	REPORT FORM
Print mailing labels	Retrieve/Label	LABEL FORM

Mathematical Calculation

Purpose	Assistant Commands	Dot Prompt Command
Calculate sum of data in field(s)	Retrieve/Sum	SUM
Calculate arithmetic mean of data in field(s)	Retrieve/Average	AVERAGE
Count number of records meeting criteria	Retrieve/Count	COUNT

Organizing Records

Purpose	Assistant Commands	Dot Prompt Command
Organize records for faster access, allowing use of SEEK command	Organize/Index	INDEX
Create new data file with records organized in order specified	Organize/Sort	SORT